USE

Renzo Piano 'Richard Rogers is a great architect. He is the only architect I know that can be a humanist at 9 o'clock in the morning, a builder at 11, a poet just before lunch and a philosopher at dinner time. This is what I call a great architect.'

FIELL

Richard Rogers
+ Architects
From the house to the city

TRANSPARENT 150

Transparency in architecture is a representation of the breakdown of traditional hierarchies, as well as opening up buildings to light and view. Layering materials allows for the play of light and shadow to be manipulated to create the impression of transparency.

SYSTEMS 174

Innovative production processes and high-tech materials that were inconceivable two decades ago have made it possible for building systems to become more flexible, adaptable and efficient. Architecture can now be the product of components made in the controlled conditions of the factory rather than on site. The discipline of such production methods gives form, scale, rhythm and legibility both to the individual parts and to the whole of a building.

URBAN 206

Compact, multi-centred cities are the only environmentally sustainable form of urban development for future generations. They are a rational and economical way of creating human settlements that offer a high quality of life. They need to combine living and work, and encourage the rich and poor, the young and old to mix freely. Pedestrians, bicycles and public transport take priority over the car, and environmental responsibility is the driving force behind the planning of such settlements.

CITIES AND THE FUTURE 226

By Richard Rogers.

WORK IN PROGRESS 228

Current and future works are featured in this section, which demonstrate how Rogers' approach is evolving as a result of the influence of his younger partners, Graham Stirk and Ivan Harbour. Within this section, the themes that define the partnership's work have been adapted to make them relevant to new demands and requirements, including climate change.

INSIDE OUT 264

Film by Marina Willer.

DIRECTORS' BIOGRAPHIES 272

MANIFESTO 277

THANK YOU 278

CREDITS 280

Rogers Stirk Harbour + Partners

1

An Evolution: Richard Rogers Partnership becomes Rogers Stirk Harbour + Partners

In 2007, Richard Rogers Partnership became Rogers Stirk Harbour + Partners (RSHP), reflecting the increasingly important role played by two of the younger directors, Graham Stirk and Ivan Harbour, alongside other established directors, like Mike Davies, Andrew Morris and Lennart Grut.

The practice's long-standing constitution and philosophy remain unaltered: RSHP continues to be owned by a charity and the directors have no financial stake in the business. But this new name signals the practice's ability to look to the future and tackle the challenges ahead – from economic uncertainty, to climate change, to affordable housing.

2

1 Rogers Stirk Harbour + Partners, 2008
2 Directors, 2009
   Standing: Andrew Morris, Lennart Grut, Graham Stirk, Ian Birtles, Mark Darbon, Ivan Harbour and Mike Davies
   Seated: Richard Rogers, Richard Paul and Amarjit Kalsi

Over more than three decades, Rogers Stirk Harbour + Partners (RSHP), has attracted critical acclaim and many international awards and honours. It has become one of the most admired architectural practices working internationally.

The practice was founded in 1977 by Richard Rogers; one of the great innovative figures of our time and in recent years has evolved as the result of his partnership with two other exceptional architects, Graham Stirk and Ivan Harbour.

The practice is best known for such pioneering buildings such as Centre Pompidou, Paris; the European Court of Human Rights, Strasbourg; Terminal 4 Barajas Airport, Madrid; and Lloyd's of London, the Millennium Dome and Lloyd's Register of Shipping, all in London.

However, Rogers is also one of the most creative thinkers in the world about the issues of urban planning and the way we need to adapt our lives and our cities to the economic and environmental challenges of the early 21st century

The work of RSHP ranges very widely to include airports, cultural projects – such as its current extension to the British Museum – hospitals, residential developments and office buildings.

Central to the philosophy of the practice is a commitment to quality in the public spaces that surround buildings, in order to ensure that inner-city areas are places that welcome the whole community. This commitment permeates all RSHP buildings, both public and private.

The practice has won many awards including, exceptionally, the Stirling Prize for Terminal 4 Barajas Airport in 2006 and again in 2009 for Maggie's London.

Richard Rogers is the 2007 Pritzker Architecture Prize Laureate, the recipient of the RIBA Gold Medal in 1985 and winner of the 1999 Thomas Jefferson Memorial Foundation Medal. His creativity burns as fiercely now as it did in those early projects conceived 40 years ago.

Sir Nicholas Serota
Director, Tate

Richard Rogers has built a reputation as one of the key architects of his generation. His designs are remarkably consistent, representing a sense of optimism about the possibilities of the modern world. For a working architect, he has taken an unusually active part in public and political life; contributing to government policy with his work on the UK's Urban Task Force, and the advocacy of high density sustainable development; and as an advisor to two successive London mayors, Ken Livingstone and Boris Johnson.

Over the last 45 years, Richard Rogers and his many colleagues and collaborators have worked to develop a shared architectural language. This is born of a fascination with the processes of construction and with the way that people relate to the buildings around them. It has sustained his architectural practice in many incarnations, firstly under the name of Team 4; then as Piano + Rogers; later as Richard Rogers Partnership; now as Rogers Stirk Harbour + Partners. The firm has a global reach, undertaking a wide range of projects from South Korea to Mexico and the USA, as well as across Europe.

This language is the product of the many people who make the practice's projects a reality. Graham Stirk and Ivan Harbour his two key present-day partners – together with other partners such as Mike Davies, John Young and Laurie Abbott – have, themselves, been intimately involved in seminal projects with Rogers that have helped to refine the subtleties of this language and created an architectural vocabulary and grammar which can be read across all work – built and unbuilt.

The practice has moved from such early speculative projects as the 'Zip-Up House', which explored how off-the-shelf components used for refrigerated containers might be put to work for prefabricated housing, to more recent attempts at approaches to low-cost housing. It has worked on high-rise office towers, airports and masterplanning projects, seen perhaps at its most developed in the competition-winning scheme for Pudong, Shanghai's new business district, and such unique projects as the Millennium Dome in London, essentially a cable-supported tent.

These themes represent an attitude to the practice of architecture as a social as well as a technical and spatial art. They are concerned not just with the creation of mute objects but with a wider understanding of the possibilities of design. Some represent the abiding values of architecture. Others are responses to a rapidly changing world. The way that the office itself is constituted and owned by a charitable trust, and Rogers' own work as an advisor on urban affairs to national governments and city mayors is another reflection of those themes. Beyond the design of individual buildings, the practice has always considered the wider urban dimension.

Public spaces are the physical realisation of society's values. Rather than creating introverted closed buildings, the practice has worked to make them permeable, bringing life to the spaces around them.

In contrast to some of the more traditional methods of the construction industry organised predominantly along craft lines, architecture can now be the product of repetitive components made in a factory. It makes the building process far more precise, and more economical. As a result, architects need to design buildings in ways that recognise this, rationalising the details, understanding structure as an assembly of carefully engineered pieces.

Rogers Stirk Harbour + Partners has a preference for lightness and transparency, rather than for the monolithic and the heavy, and not just for aesthetic reasons. In the past, architecture has been used to represent traditional hierarchies. Transparency breaks these hierarchies down, as well as opening up buildings to light and view. Legibility in architecture finds order, scale and expression in the process of construction. The practice designs buildings that make it clear how they work, and how they are made. Structure is exposed and visible, each element in a building such as stairs and services is articulated.

For many years, the practice has worked to promote the idea of compact, multi-centred cities as the only sustainable form for urban development. Such cities make the best use of scarce land and can support efficient public transport systems. They are also more likely to encourage the kind of rich social diversity that is the mark of a flourishing city.

Lightweight structures achieve more with less material. It's a strategy that reflects an attitude to the careful use of resources, and is the route to an elegant economy of means. Sustainability has been an essential quality since the early days. 'Green' implies buildings and cities that are designed to be environmentally responsible. It is not about a style.

Until modern times, successful human settlements have always been based on environmental balance. Cheap energy upset that balance. Architects are now obliged to redress the imbalance, using means that range from the passive to the technological.

Richard Rogers was shaped in part by his family background, the product of an Anglo-Italian upbringing. His cousin, Ernesto Rogers, was a member of the celebrated Milanese practice

BBPR, that built the Torre Velesca in Milan. As editor of Domus magazine, he wrote the famous editorial in 1946 which suggested that from a close enough examination of a spoon, it would be possible to understand the nature of the kind of city that the culture that created it would build. Richard Rogers has always subscribed to this idea. In essence, he believes that there is a kind of design DNA running through projects at every scale, and perhaps also, that it is the connection between architecture and the people who use it which is essential to bringing it to life.

Rogers was born in Florence, Italy in 1933, but moved to England as a child. He was educated at the Architectural Association in London in the decade following World War Two. He was taught, among others, by Alan Colquhoun and then went through the transforming experience of a postgraduate year at Yale. In America he was exposed at first hand to the work of Frank Lloyd Wright, Louis Kahn, and Charles Eames. He was a student of Paul Rudolph, who gave him a crash course in form shaping; of the historian Vincent Scully; and of Serge Chermayeff, who provided him with an insight into the sociology of city planning. James Stirling was a visiting tutor.

Yale was also the place where he got to know Norman Foster. After graduating and a spell working for SOM in San Francisco, Rogers went home to start his first practice Team 4 with Norman and Wendy Foster and Su Rogers, his first wife. In the brief life of Team 4, they completed Creek Vean. This is a remarkable private house that owed much to Rogers' experiences of America where he and Foster – under the spell of the inspirational teaching of Scully – had visited every Frank Lloyd Wright building that they could find. While travelling around the States, Rogers was also greatly influenced by visiting Charles and Ray

Eames' house in Santa Monica, and other great modern buildings such as Rudolph Schindler's Chase House in West Hollywood and Raphael Soriano's Shulman House.

Team 4's largest work was Reliance Controls, the now demolished factory outside Swindon that drew on the precedents of Charles Eames and the work of the Southern California Schools System to produce Britain's first 'high-tech' building. The building was characterised by diagonal cross-braced structure and exposed steel I-beams.

After Team 4, Rogers established his own practice under the wing of the Design Research Unit, the design consultancy started by his father-in-law, Marcus Brumwell, also the client for the Creek Vean house. They built a roof-top extension to accommodate the studio in Aybrook Street, in London's Marylebone. This was memorialised by Jan Kaplicky, Rogers' one-time assistant, with a montage that showed a VW Beetle plugged into the building's roof. What happened next was what made Rogers' name, and laid the foundations for the practice as it is today. Almost as soon as Rogers had established a practice with Renzo Piano, they entered – much against Rogers' better judgment – the competition to build a new arts centre in the middle of Paris.

Modernism looked exhausted in the 1970s, but the Pompidou Centre in Paris re-energised it. Some 30 years after its completion, the Pompidou is still an extraordinary achievement; a tour de force in the manipulation of construction and materials, inspired in part by the work of Jean Prouvé, who was in fact the chairman of the competition jury, and also, perhaps, by the counter-cultural flamboyance of the period. The Pompidou could be seen as the progeny not just of Prouvé's meticulous, deft engineering and

making, but also of the impermanence of Cedric Price's architectural projections and the playful anarchy of Archigram. But unlike either of them, the Rogers' team was able to go through with the project, and actually build what seemed like an impossible vision at the outset.

Rogers and Piano went their separate ways after the Pompidou was completed. Rogers' practice explored some of the themes suggested by the Pompidou in the Lloyd's of London building. These are buildings which are highly legible: the way that they work is made visible, with a structural system clearly articulated; there is a clear distinction between served and servant space, in the manner of Louis Kahn who had inspired Rogers as a student.

When the climate against experiment and innovative architecture hardened in the 1980s, Rogers refused to compromise. He maintained his approach and his design philosophy.

Today the practice is busy across the world, taking part in the reconstruction of the former World Trade Center site in Manhattan, New York, as well as working on projects in Japan, China and Australia and across Europe on architectural and masterplanning schemes.

Deyan Sudjic
Director, Design Museum, London

I have always liked mechanical things. One of the first toys that I can remember playing with in Italy was Meccano.

Architecture is about celebration. Obviously if there is nothing to celebrate then it is no longer architecture, it is just construction.

Mechanics has an inherent beauty which we manipulate. This is how we get our aesthetics and make it a primary part of our expression.

As architects, we use technology to solve social problems and to give form. Otherwise, we would end up with structures which are nothing to do with architecture. It's that marriage, the juxtaposition between the frame, the infill, the mechanical system and movement – that is what gives a building meaning and legibility. This is then manipulated in terms of scale, colour and form all of which create a language. That is really what architecture is about.

EXPO

Richard Rogers

Our buildings are more like carefully-designed, indeterminate robots than frozen temples. Flexibility to meet the changing needs of a building over time is key to our design approach.

In composing the form of a building, we use technology and art, and the play of light and shadow on form. By manipulating and giving order to technology and the construction process, we give form. We create an alphabet of technology with parts made up of grain, order, scale, style and poetry and the use of different colours to create fun and serious moods. We build up a narrative and a 'language mode' comparable to words, sentences and paragraphs in grammar.

Film direction: Marina Willer
and Seonaid Mackay
Production: Beatrice Vears
Duration: 5'37"

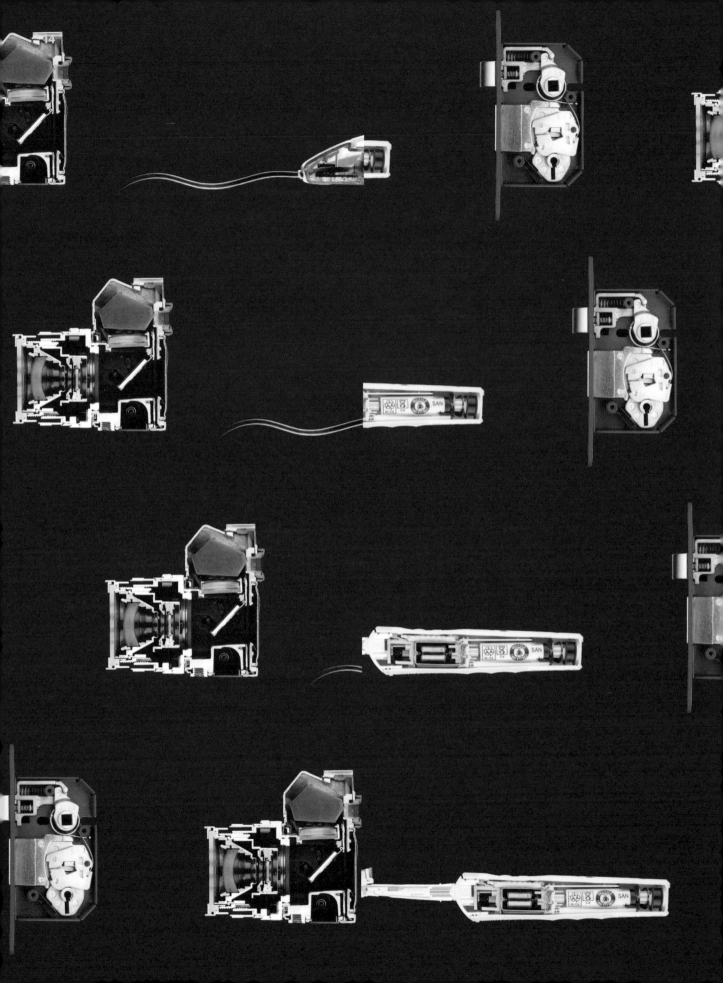

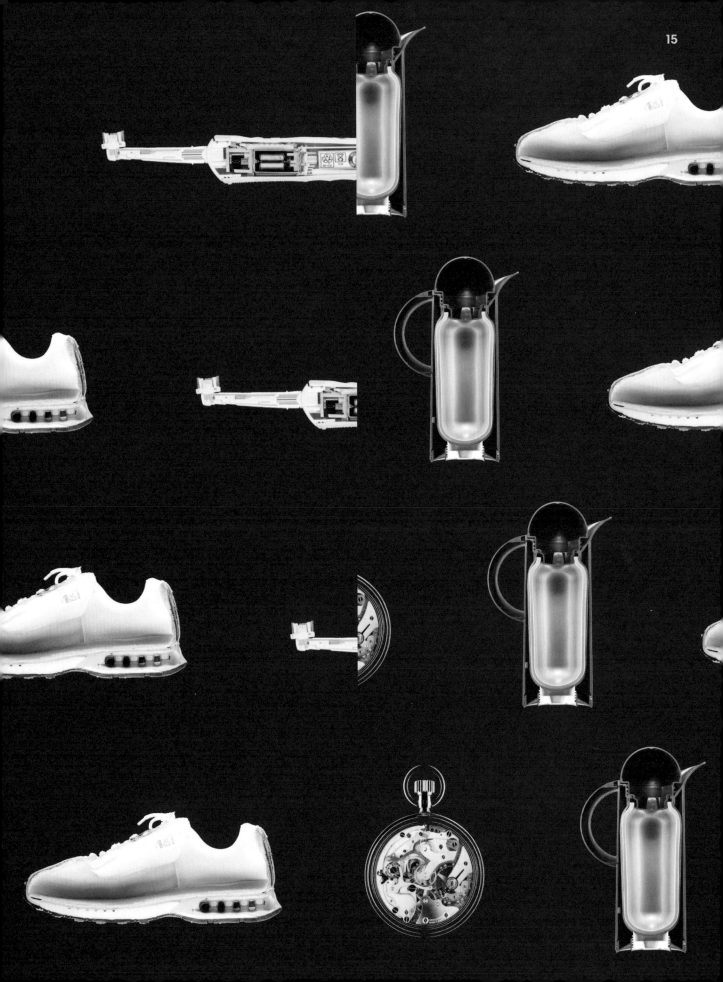

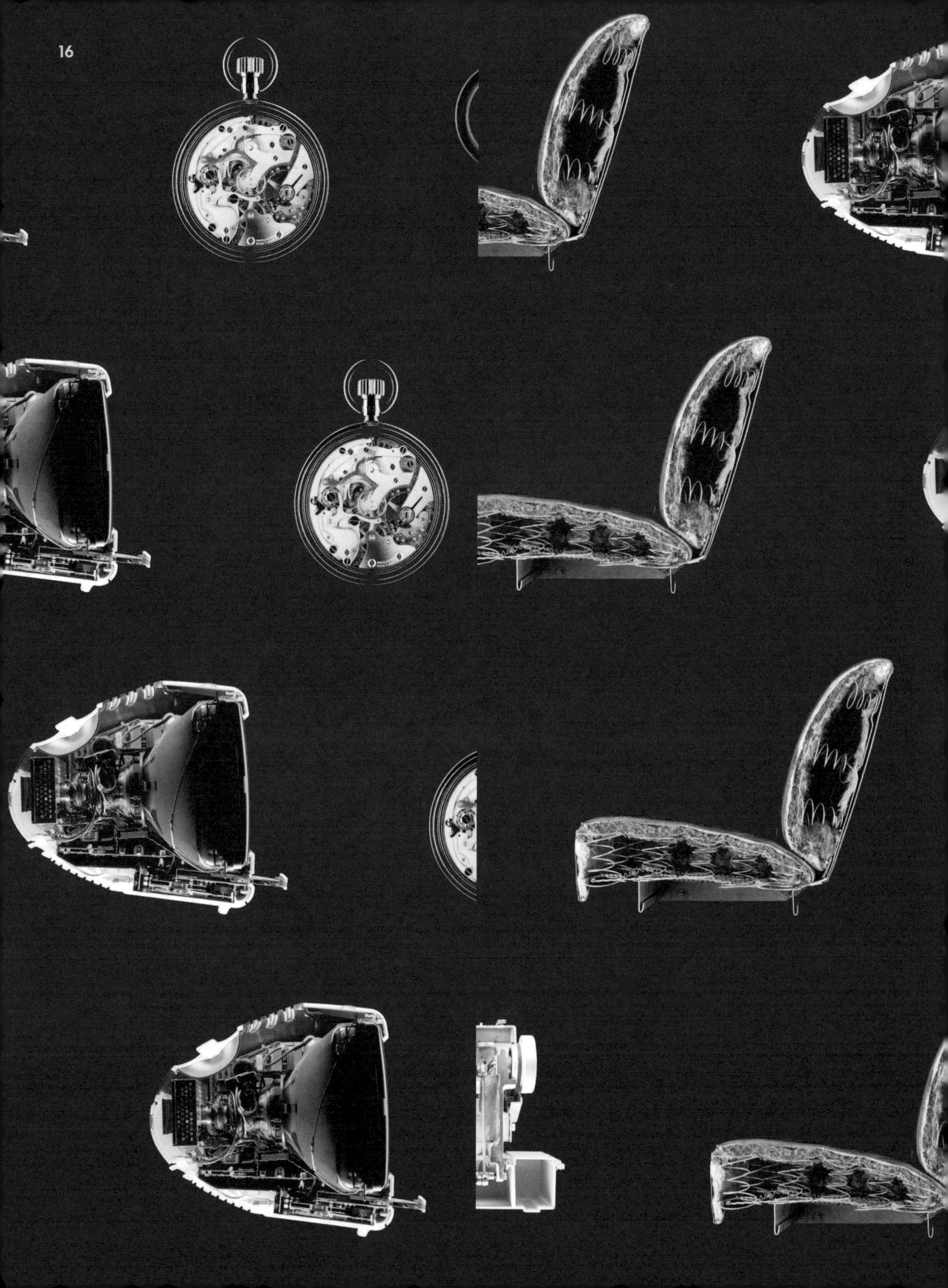

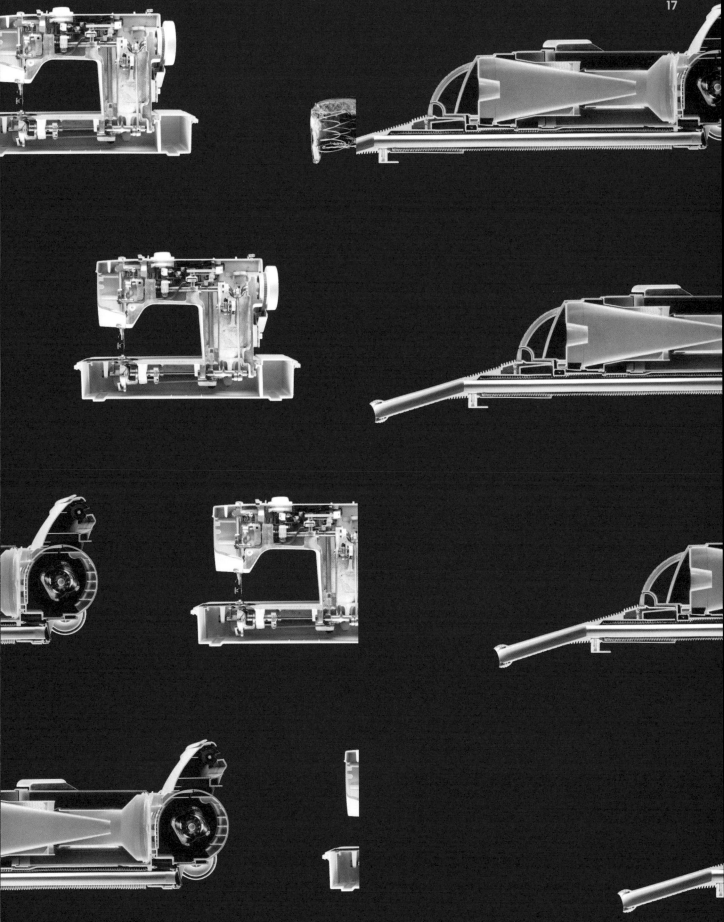

EA
WC

RLY
ORK

This section highlights projects undertaken by Richard Rogers as part of Team 4 (with Norman and Wendy Foster and Su Rogers). It explores the early theories applied in Rogers' works including flexibility, legibility and the research and use of new production processes as can be seen in the Zip-Up House and the Rogers' House. It provides a fascinating insight into Rogers' early thinking on the organisation of work and living space and the ability of buildings to adapt to changing requirements over time. Many of the projects in this section hint at the boldness of the Pompidou Centre and Lloyd's of London and demonstrate an awareness and application of new materials in construction that was years ahead of its time.

Early Works

Film direction and Production: hijack. Duration: 9'34"

My parents were Italian and coming to England on the eve of the Second World War was difficult. Not only could I not speak the language, but Italians were not popular in 1939. At school, my aim was to be second from bottom rather than bottom of the class. Later, I found out I was dyslexic.

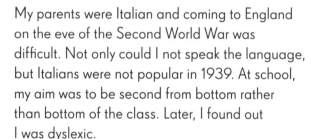

My father was a doctor and my mother a potter and artist. Growing up, I was very conscious of the political and social environment that forced my parents out of Italy. Science, art and politics are what drive me today.

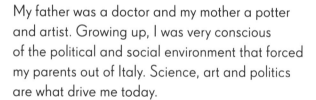

In the 'Early Works' film which is part of the 'Richard Rogers + Architects: From the House to the City' exhibition, Richard Rogers discusses his formative years as an architect and some of his key influences.

Ernesto Rogers

Ernesto was a great humanist, teacher, author and architect, perhaps one of the most important architects in Italy in the period following the Second World War.

Post-war

In the post-war period, British art and architecture suffered from what is commonly called 'The Shock of the New'. The Festival of Britain – which I visited in 1951 – was an enlightening moment. The 'Dome of Discovery' and the 'Skylon' combined both science and art. It was a very exciting time. Suddenly, The Festival of Britain showed us the potential of seeing what the world could be like ... a window into the future.

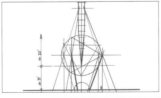

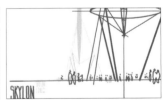

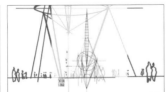

It was during my stay in the States in 1960 – 2 with my first wife, Su, and Norman Foster that I began to formulate a more personal vision of what architecture was about. I had some exceptional tutors such as Vincent Scully, Paul Rudolph and Serge Chermayeff. Even more important was the influence of those wonderful buildings by Frank Lloyd Wright, Louis Kahn, Mies van der Rohe, Rudolph Schindler, Raphael Soriano and, in particular, the lightweight structures of the Case Study Houses in California. But perhaps the greatest influence on my work was meeting Norman Foster at Yale where we studied for our Masters.

Maison de Verre

A building which has greatly influenced me is the Maison de Verre in Paris. It has a magical interior of interlocking spaces – tailor-made mobile partitions within an elegant steel framework – flooded by light through a translucent glass brick façade.

We tend to embrace the use of colour as one of the ways to strengthen the 'mood' of our buildings... colour also helps to emphasise certain rhythms, geometries and scales.

Team 4

I left Yale in the early 60's and set up Team 4 with Su, my wife and with Norman and Wendy Foster. The first building we worked on was Creek Vean in Cornwall which still very much demonstrates the influence of Frank Lloyd Wright. The Reliance Controls factory – now demolished – was the only other building of our partnership, but it set the tone for much of our future work.

Collaboration

Over the years, I have had the good fortune to work with a large number of different designers, consultants and clients, collaborating with people with a variety of skills.

I have worked with many very talented people such as Norman Foster, Peter Rice and Renzo Piano. I knew about Renzo's work before I met him. We both were very interested in lightweight, moveable structures, in open frameworks rather than closed buildings, in the use of construction processes to give scale and rhythm to buildings.

John Young, the partner who I worked with for nearly all my professional life, has a fantastic ability to design and manipulate components and to create poetry out of technology. Mike Davies is a visionary, a person who can grapple with spatial concepts at a global scale. Laurie Abbott is a brilliant designer and technician.

I have worked with Graham Stirk and Ivan Harbour for more than 25 years. They are exceptionally talented designers who will lead the practice into the future.

Pompidou Centre

For two architects in their 30s, to win the Pompidou Centre competition was like winning the lottery! We had a shared vision of what the building should be – both in social and architectural terms – a place for people of all ages, all creeds, for young and old. At the heart of the project is the public domain, extending from the great piazza at the front of the building and continuing up the face of the building with its 'streets in the air' and escalators snaking up the façades. The mechanical services were placed on the opposite side of the building, allowing the creation of uninterrupted floors and offering maximum flexibility for change over time.

Rogers' House

This house, built for Rogers' parents, consists of two single-storey pavilions arranged within a garden plot.

The concept was for the house to be assembled rather than built. The framework consists of eight steel portals, three for the studio and five for the main house, with a central garden courtyard that could be filled in to link the buildings if required. The internal divisions and utilities are designed for maximum adaptability – the side walls are of plastic-coated aluminium panels joined with a neoprene 'zip' system.

The colourful internal areas alternate with the comparatively muted colours of the gardens to create a progression of spaces that erodes the distinction between 'inside' and 'outside' – garden, house, courtyard, studio.

Rogers has described the design of the house as a 'transparent, flexible tube with solid walls only on the boundary, which could be adapted, extended, or completely opened up.' The house has proved its flexibility: it is now home to one of Rogers' sons, Ab, and his young family.

London, UK, 1968 – 9 (built)
Client: Nino and Dada Rogers
Architect: Richard + Su Rogers

1

Richard Rogers 'The whole house was designed as a transparent, flexible tube which could be adapted and extended, or completely opened up to involve everyone – guests, friends and family. The close relationship between the house, the garden, Ernesto Rogers' furniture and Dada Rogers' pottery made this perhaps the most successful small project I have been involved in.'

2

1 Richard Rogers' sketch shows the connection of the house to Wimbledon Common.
2 Boundary walls use prefabricated, storey-height, insulated panels.
3 Night-time view showing house within its mature suburban garden.

3

4

5

6

4 – 7   The interior of the house is furnished with an
eclectic mix of items including designs by Ernesto
Rogers and pottery by Dada Rogers (above).

7

8 – 10 Interior of house as it is now for Ab Rogers
and his family.
11 Ab, Sophie, Ella and Lula Rogers.
12 View from garden showing the openness
and transparency of the Rogers' House.

9

10

11

12

Zip-Up House

The Zip-Up House shows how householders can be offered choice and control over their living environment, while minimising construction, maintenance and running costs and providing a model of environmental efficiency. It was designed in response to 'The House for Today' competition.

The Zip-Up House is quickly assembled from mass-produced parts – panels designed for refrigerated trucks and draft-proof windows created for buses – which can be bought as kits and fastened together using neoprene zips. New modules can be added, and the lack of fixed walls within the house allows the internal layout to adapt quickly to the changing requirements of its inhabitants.

The house can be assembled, extended and changed at a fraction of the cost and time required for a conventional building. The steel jacks that support the building enable it to be freed from the constraints of land contours. Running costs are also minimised – the structural panels give an insulation value seven times that of a traditional house of the time, and a three-bedroom house can be heated by a 3 kW heater.

No. 1: 1968 (unbuilt)
No. 2: 1971 (prototype)
Client: Various
Architect: Team 4

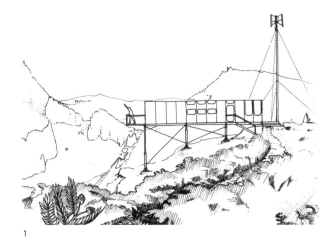

1

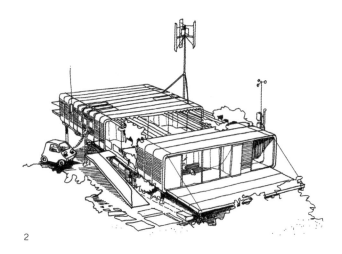

2

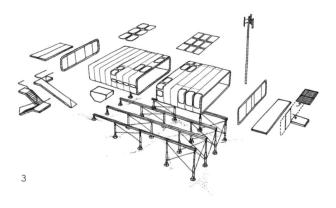

3

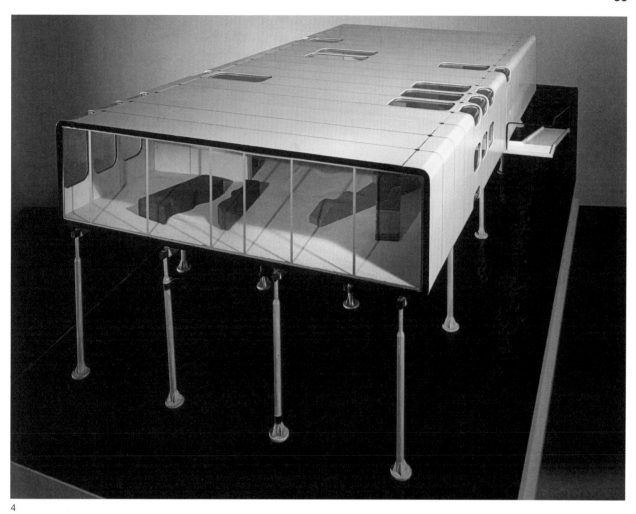

4

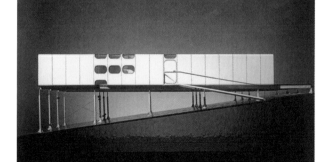

5

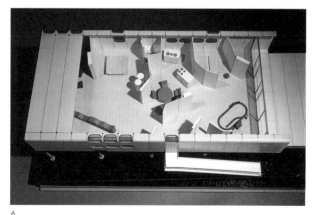

6

1 Elevation showing Zip-Up House on sloping site.
2 Zip-Up House with battery-operated
  car and wind turbine.
3 Prefabricated components of Zip-Up House.
4–6 Model, scale 1:20.

PUB

BLIC

An unbroken urban tradition linking the Parthenon in Athens, the Campo in Siena, and London's Trafalgar Square, reflects the balance between community life and private privilege. Flourishing public spaces reflect a flourishing society.

The greatest challenge for an architect is to design buildings that can bring life to the cities around them. It's a goal that has been at the heart of the work of Rogers' practice for 40 years. This is nowhere more evident than in the Place Beaubourg. In Piano and Rogers' submission for the Pompidou Centre competition, the space in front of the building was described as 'a place for all people, all ages, all creeds, a cross between the British Museum and Times Square.' It has become just that. The building was integrated with the piazza, with public space continuing up the escalators and out onto open terraces.

Public spaces are the physical realisation of a society's values. They are shaped by the communities that use them, which in turn are shaped by the spaces that define them. Public space is a catalyst, generating energy and excitement. It also brings a calm and stillness that offers a respite from the noise and chaos of cities.

Pompidou Centre

The Pompidou Centre brought Richard Rogers and Renzo Piano international fame. Working with Arup – led by the engineer Peter Rice – to a brief that required an arts centre, a museum of modern art, a library, and music research centres, a democratic fun palace for the information age was created.

The scale of the site offered scope to create a stage for civic life in the Marais, one of the most deprived areas in Paris. The design is based on continuous public space: the large public piazza in front of the building continues vertically up its façade, where snaking escalators create streets in the air.

Brightly coloured and richly detailed services are aligned along the rue du Renard. Together with the building's exposed steel superstructure, this design creates a richly articulated exterior, allows for highly flexible uninterrupted floorplates nearly 50 m deep and 180 m long, and fosters transparency, from the edge of the piazza to the depths of the building.

Standing out from and complementing its urban context, the Pompidou Centre met a national need for an iconic cultural centre, and has performed a local function as a catalyst for regeneration, drawing people from all walks of life back to the Marais.

Paris, France, 1971 – 7 (built)
Client: French Government
Architect: Piano + Rogers

1

1 Site before development.
2 Aerial view in its urban context.
3 Section from rue du Renard.
4 Floor plan.

2

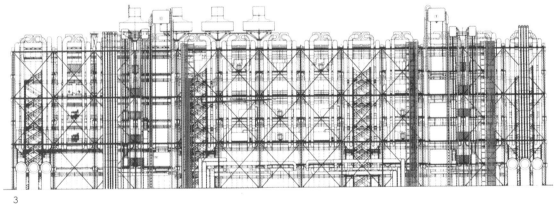

3

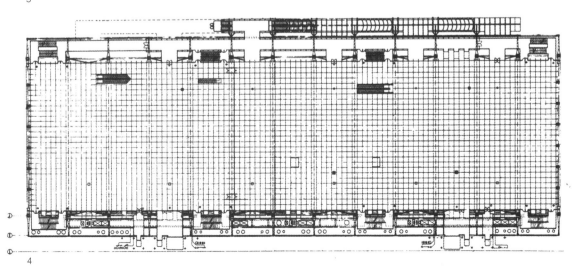

4

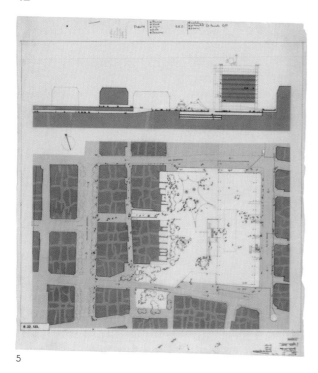

5

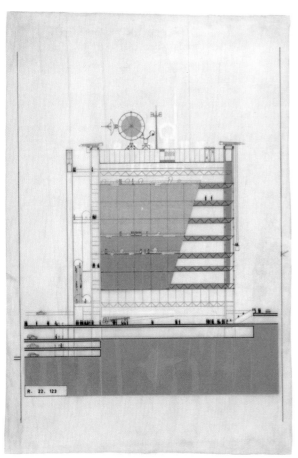

6

Richard Rogers 'Beaubourg was conceived as a live centre of information and entertainment – a flexible container and a dynamic communications machine, highly serviced and made from prefabricated parts. Cutting across traditional institutional limits, we created a vibrant meeting place where activities would overlap in flexible, well serviced spaces, a people's centre, a university of the street reflecting the constantly changing needs of its users – a place for all people of all ages, all creeds.'

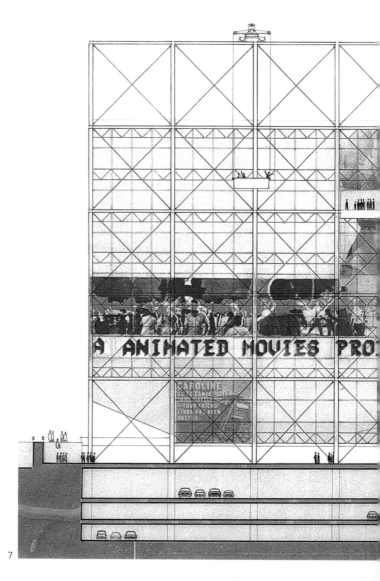

7

5 Competition drawing (plan).
6 Competition drawing (section).
7 Piazza elevation for competition entry illustrating the concept of the building as an information centre.
8 Philip Johnson chooses the winning competition entry.

8

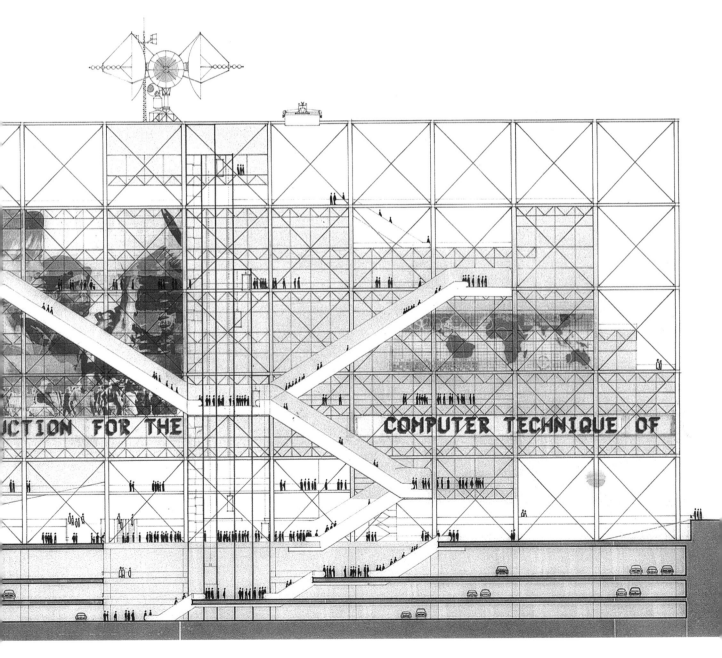

...CTION FOR THE   COMPUTER TECHNIQUE OF

9

10

11

9 Gerberettes under construction.
10 Assembling the structural frame.
11 Construction worker with gerberette.

13

12 Detail of piazza façade
  showing main entrance
  and escalator (page left).
13 Detail of escalator looking
  down to Beaubourg.
14 Detail of services.

14

'Richard Rogers + Architects: From the House to the City'
–The exhibition on display at the Pompidou Centre,
November 2007 – February 2008.

National Gallery Extension

In 1981, the UK Government launched a competition to create additional space for the National Gallery.

Rogers' proposal consists of top-lit galleries elevated on slender columns above a separate office building. The floor plan of the gallery has no fixed internal divisions, and the roof lighting system matches this flexibility, using a complex system of louvres to re-direct daylight as needed.

To one side, a tower housing a restaurant and viewing gallery acts as a counterpoint to the steeple of St Martin's-in-the-Fields Church on the other side of Trafalgar Square. The gallery itself is connected to street level via a free-standing ramp, with additional towers for services and escape routes.

The scheme also proposes a strategy for public space. At the time, it was not considered possible to close the busy road that separated the National Gallery and Trafalgar Square, so the scheme includes an underground galleria, linking the National Gallery to Leicester Square and Trafalgar Square, thereby offering improved pedestrian access in one of London's key cultural and tourist areas.

London, UK, 1982 (unbuilt)
Client: The National Gallery

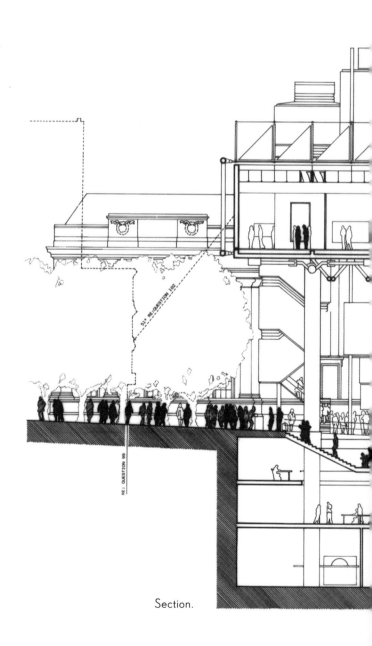

Section.

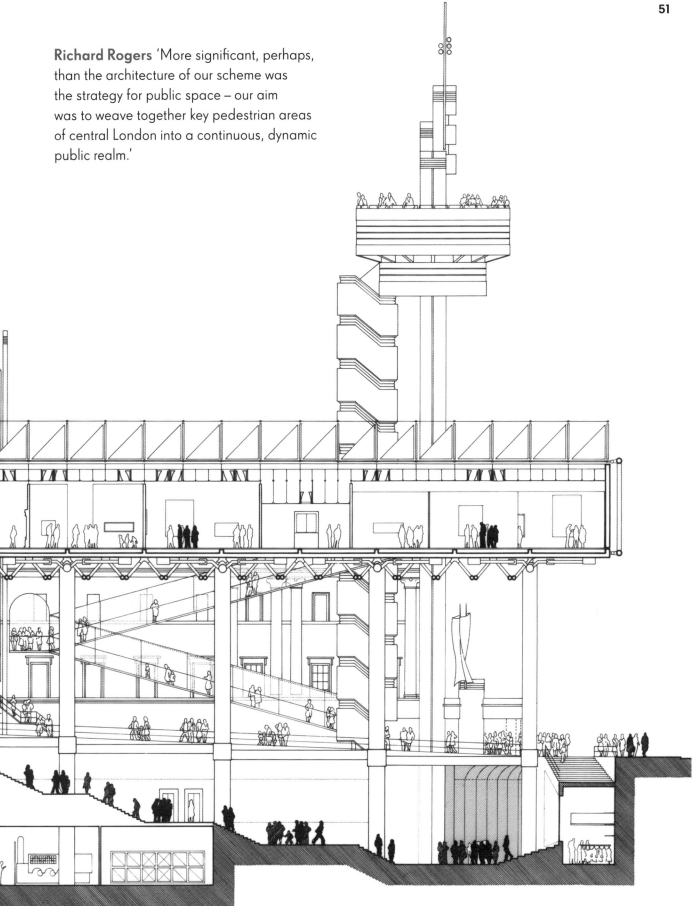

Richard Rogers 'More significant, perhaps, than the architecture of our scheme was the strategy for public space – our aim was to weave together key pedestrian areas of central London into a continuous, dynamic public realm.'

2 Site plan.
3 Detail showing underpass linking
   National Gallery with Trafalgar Square.
4 Section from Trafalgar Square.
5 Scheme model, scale 1:500.
6 Model of public piazza, scale 1:100.

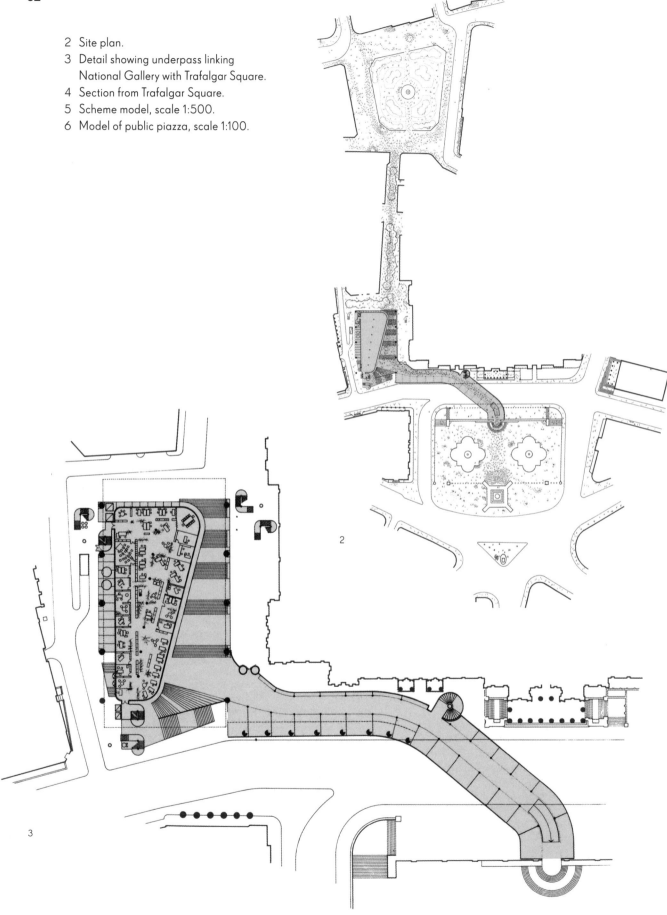

2

3

4

5

6

Tokyo International Forum

The brief for this site, surrounded by busy city streets and a railway viaduct in the commercial heart of Tokyo, required three multi-purpose halls, the largest of which had to seat 4,000 people.

The response was to turn away from the traditional, internalised, design of performance spaces to create a transparent and accessible public forum at ground level, as a place for people to meet and a refuge from the hectic city streets.

The three auditoria are suspended above this naturally-ventilated space, like three huge steel ship hulls – supported by a fixed frame of steel portals – which also accommodate services and escape systems. Topped with roof gardens, cafés and restaurants, the halls are connected to the ground level by escalators floating through space.

Like the Pompidou Centre, this scheme was conceived as an urban landscape in microcosm, creating a new 'piece of city' and providing a continuous public realm, with enhanced links to adjacent rail and underground stations as well as to surrounding streets.

Tokyo, Japan, 1990 (unbuilt)
Client: Mitsubishi

1

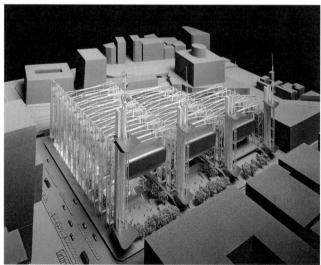

2

1 & 2 Competition model, scale 1:500.
   3 Section through the three auditoria.
   4 Section through auditorium.

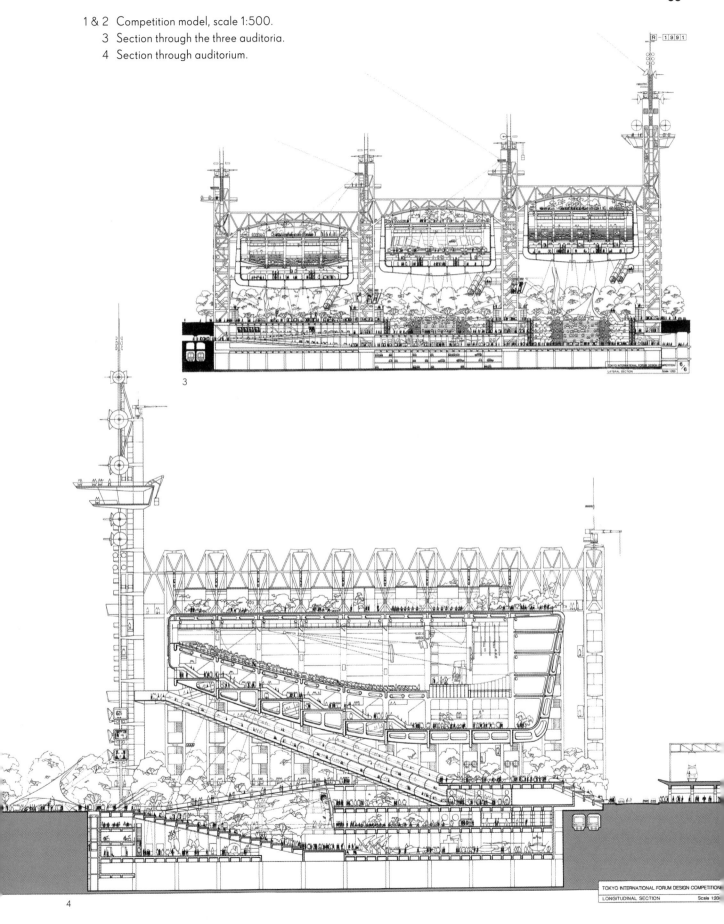

3

4

South Bank Centre

London, UK, 1994 – 7 (unbuilt)
Client: Arts Council / South Bank Centre

This scheme sought to bring civic life back to
the South Bank Centre, the complex of post-war
cultural buildings on the south bank of the River
Thames – London's greatest and yet most
neglected public space.

In response to a 1994 competition, Rogers
proposed a new 'Crystal Palace', a glass roof
in the form of a wave, designed with Arup. This
would replace the existing elevated walkways,
and enclose and give unity to the tough 1960s
buildings of the existing centre, at the same time
as connecting these to the Royal Festival Hall,
to a new performance space and to the rest
of central London.

The wave roof would also accommodate shops
and restaurants, and create an environment
in which street life could flourish all year round,
without artificial heating or cooling.

1

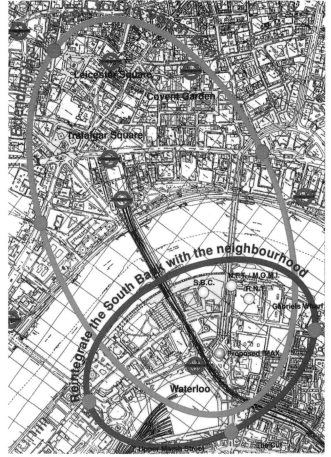

2

3

1 Site.
2 Diagram showing connections to South Bank
  from West End of London.
3 Proposed scheme.

Computer-generated image of proposed
scheme from the River Thames.

Ivan Harbour 'This scheme is about reinvigorating London's performing arts centre, integrating it with its neighbourhood and the West End.'

Rome Congress Centre

Rome, Italy, 1999 (unbuilt)
Client: Centro Congressi Italia

This competition scheme was designed for a site in the EUR district of Rome, an area planned in the 1930s according to the rigidly formalistic urbanism of the fascist era.

The scheme sets the main congress and exhibition areas in a cantilevered roof space, supported by central columns and surrounded by service towers. A wide public terrace runs round the edge of the roof, optimising views across the Rome skyline.

Beneath the great over-sailing, timber-clad roof is a second building for offices, ticket areas, restaurants, parking, shops and a hotel, its roof forming a wedge-shaped ramp of public space.

The public nature of the building is emphasised by the provision of a partially enclosed 2,000-seat amphitheatre within the lower building, alongside which runs a new pedestrian route, linking the EUR Fermi Station with the existing Palazzo dei Congressi. Further shops are placed alongside this route, and around the edge of the building, to ensure an open relationship with the public domain.

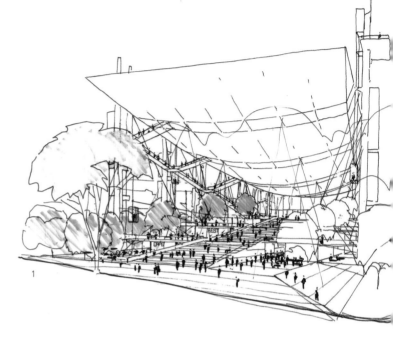

1

2

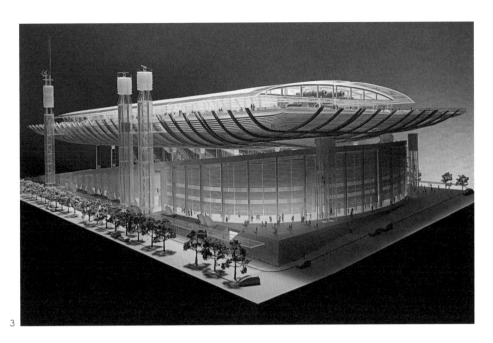

3

1 Sketch showing public access.
2 & 3 Competition model, scale 1:200.

Maggie's London

London, UK, 2001 – 8 (built)
Client: Maggie's

Inspired by the late Maggie Keswick, and
her husband, the landscape designer and
architectural critic and writer, Charles Jencks,
this is the latest in a chain of cancer caring
centres built by voluntary fundraising, and
designed by distinguished architects who have
donated their services. Based in the grounds
of the Charing Cross Hospital (the practice's
local hospital), the centre provides advice and
support for people affected by cancer whether
patients, family or friends. The attribute of
the raised roof allows natural light to enter the
internal space of the centre and partitions divide
up the open structure inside placing the kitchen
at the heart of the building. It is conceived as
a welcoming and inviting refuge with an open,
domestic atmosphere.

Main entrance.

Ivan Harbour 'Maggie's London needed to create its own sequence of internal and external environments – a welcoming beacon in this busy London streetscape.'

2 View through window into kitchen area (above).
3 Ground floor plan.
4 Kitchen area.
5 Library area.

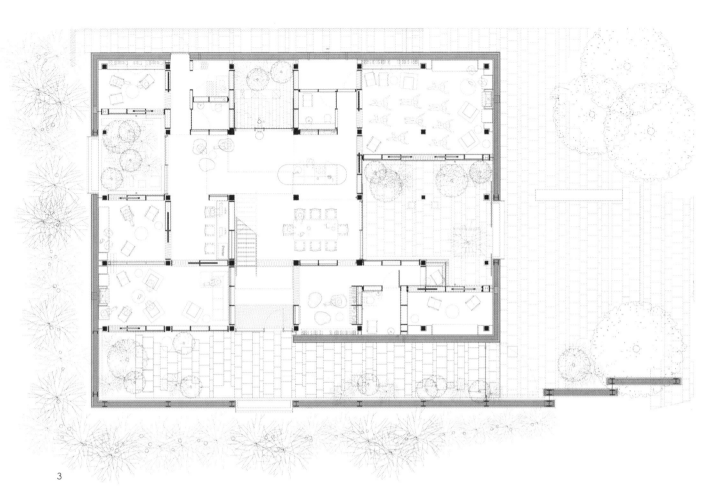

3

4

5

6

6 Landscaped courtyard for meetings.
7 Roof detail (page right).

LEG

IBLE

Legibility in architecture finds order and expression in the process of construction. Lloyd's of London, the headquarters of the world's oldest insurance market, is a clearly articulated building which reflects the way in which it was made, what makes it stand up, and how it works. This layering is both a functional and a visual issue. It creates an architectural grain that animates the building both at a distance as an element in the city, and close up. It is the embodiment of Louis Kahn's ideas about 'served and servant spaces.'

A series of towers on the perimeter house those elements that are subject to regular change – lifts, stairs, services and toilet pods – while also giving grain and shadow to the building.

The concept of legibility can be understood as an attempt to make visible the activities that take place inside a building, to give them an identity, rather than leaving them as anonymous functions within uniform blocks.

Lloyd's of London

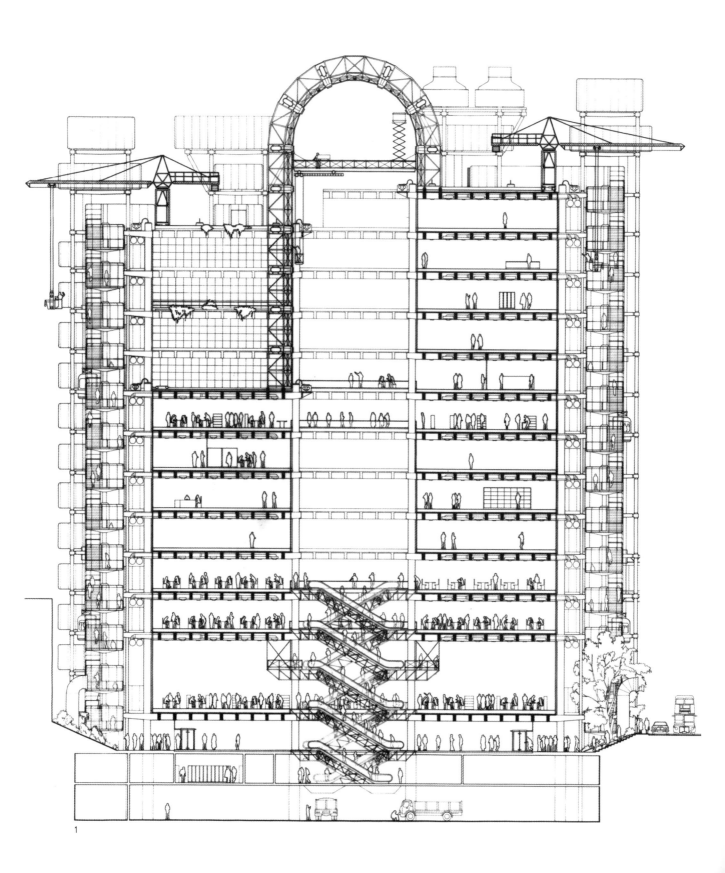

1

Location: London, UK, 1978 – 86 (built)
Client: Lloyd's

Lloyd's of London, one of the world's leading insurance markets, has its origins nearly 300 years ago in a London coffee house. By the late 1970s, after three moves in 50 years, Lloyd's wanted flexible space that enabled underwriters and brokers to continue to meet face-to-face, while providing up-to-date office space.

The core of the building is a 14-storey arched atrium, around which are grouped galleries that can be adapted for use as a trading area for underwriters or as private offices. To enable this flexibility and transparency, the building's services are concentrated in irregularly spaced towers at the perimeter of the building.

The building steps up from the low historic buildings on the south to higher office buildings behind, and is articulated by the service towers and the atrium's glazed, arched roof.

The service towers, remodelled to accommodate the growing demands of IT infrastructure, bridge the gap between a rectangular building and the irregular boundary defined by the City of London's medieval street patterns.

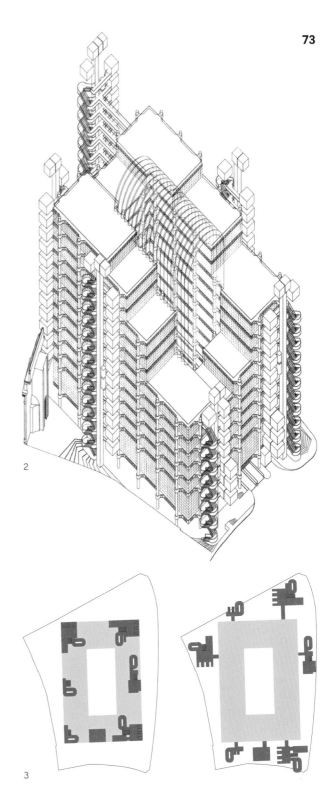

2

3

1 Cross section through the atrium.
2 The form of the building.
3 Comparison showing traditional service core arrangements (left) and those at Lloyd's of London (right).

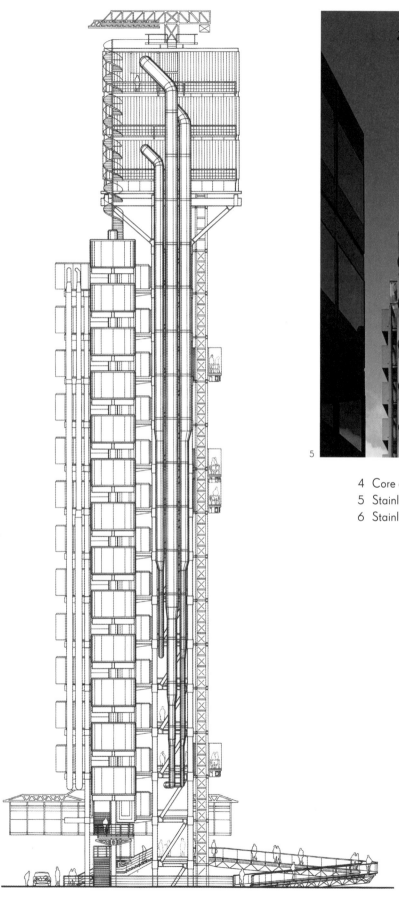

5

4 Core elevation.
5 Stainless steel services and core.
6 Stainless steel service risers and toilet capsules.

4

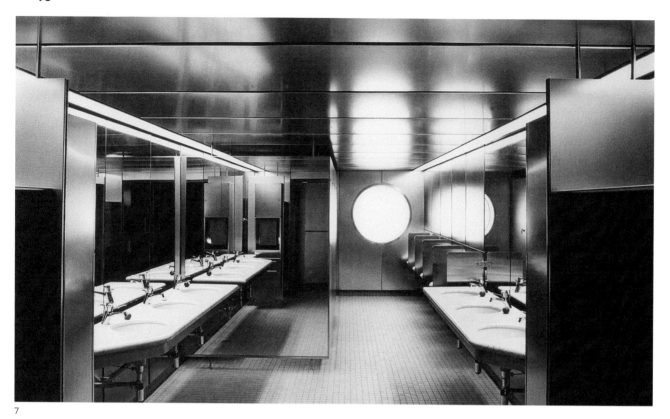

7

7 Toilet capsule interior.
8 Prefabricated toilet capsule being
   craned into place.
9 Dimpled steel rollers used to pattern glass.
10 Molten glass passed through rollers
   to create textured surface.
11 Finished textured glass that reflects
   and refracts light.
12 Glass is used in office space to create
   light and shade.

8

9

10

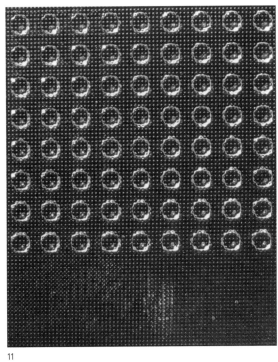

11

12

14

13 Interior view of atrium.
14 'The Room' showing escalators.

15

John Young 'Turning the plan inside out by placing service cores outside the main envelope offers two principal benefits – freeing the building of all internal obstructions, and making lifts and servicing systems more accessible for maintenance and future upgrades without disturbance to the occupants.'

15 & 16 The 'Gothic' character of Lloyd's is particularly appropriate to the medieval street pattern of the City of London.

Kabuki-Cho

Tokyo, Japan, 1987 – 93 (built)
Client: K-One Corporation
Co-architect: Architect 5

Kabuki-Cho, the first of Rogers' buildings to be constructed in Japan, was originally envisaged as a hotel scheme, but subsequently re-designed as an annexe to a neighbouring office building. The building is located within the tight-knit streets of the Shinjuku commercial district of Tokyo, and the need to safeguard existing rights of light was paramount.

The 12-storey building is set back from the street and allows light into its two basement storeys (which contain a restaurant), through a dramatic glazed roof that sweeps up four storeys from the pavement. Above this roof, four storeys are cantilevered out, further optimising the use of space and light.

The frame is constructed of steel combined with concrete (to meet local fire safety and seismic regulations), and this defines the main floor spaces of the building. A 'servant' tower contains lifts, lavatories and other services. Kabuki-Cho, which used both British and Japanese craftsmen in its construction, creates a modern, social space in the heart of a traditional city district.

Laurie Abbott 'The building's form was entirely dictated by planning constraints and rights of light – its profile and area conform exactly to the available light cones.'

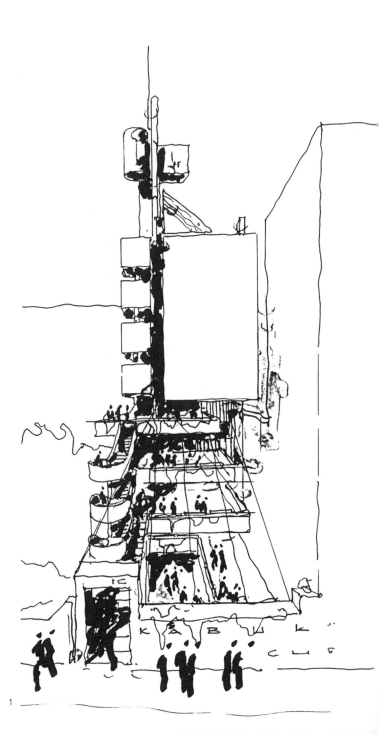

1

2

1 Sketch of initial hotel design.
2 Profile of building is determined
   by rights-of-light requirements.

3

4

5

6

3 – 7 Great attention was paid to the detailing of the façade, using repetitive functional elements to define the lightweight language of the building.

Tomigaya Exhibition Building

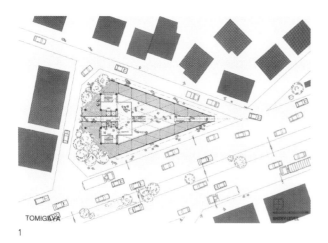

1

Tokyo, Japan, 1990 – 2 (unbuilt)
Client: Soichi Hisaeda

The client's brief called for a landmark structure on this tiny triangular site surrounded by low-rise housing, a park and a busy highway. While a building height of 45 m was permissible, the building was only allowed to have three floors.

The practice explored with the client the potential of a vertical exhibition space, plus a limited area for offices, with transparent floors visible from the highway.

Two main steel trusses, hung from the principal supporting towers, define the triangular glazed space at the public heart of the building. Stairs, lifts and other services are relegated to the rear in a zone between the towers.

The trusses also support a large crane that can be used to lift and reposition the movable mezzanine floors depending on the requirements of particular exhibitions, allowing exhibits as large as a yacht or a helicopter to be displayed across different floors.

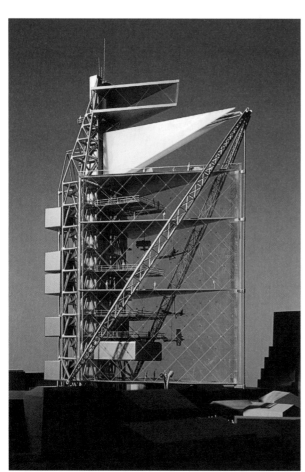

2

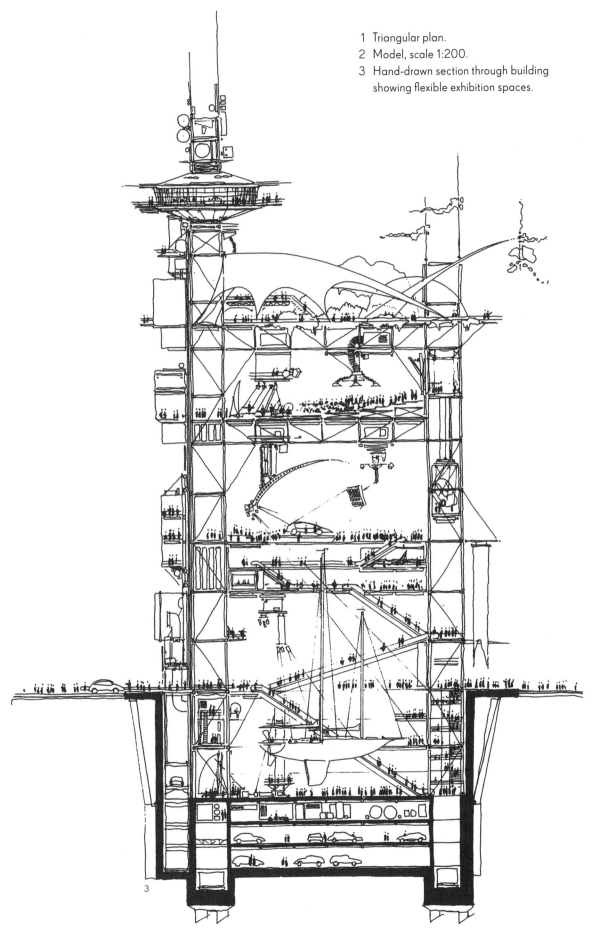

1 Triangular plan.
2 Model, scale 1:200.
3 Hand-drawn section through building showing flexible exhibition spaces.

3

LIGHTV

VEIGHT

The economical enclosure of space has been fundamental to the visions of engineers for two centuries, as seen in the great iron and glass railway termini of the 19th century. In the 20th century, Jean Prouvé, Buckminster Fuller and Pierre Chareau explored ever more elegant ways of using as little steel as possible to achieve as much as they could, in opposition to the architectural tradition of massive, solid, load-bearing walls.

Rogers' practice is firmly in the lightness camp, consistently seeking to find the maximum economy of means – doing more with less through close interaction with engineers. The result is an architecture that is lightweight and which responds to functional needs.

A series of projects reflects this theme, from the minimal enclosure of the Reliance Controls factory, where the slender structure was stabilised by diagonal braces, to the Millennium Dome – essentially a cable-supported tent spanning huge distances with the minimum of structure.

INMOS Microprocessor Factory

The INMOS scheme began as a design for a model microchip factory, which could be built quickly (operational within a year of start on site) in a wide variety of locations, and could be expanded or otherwise adapted without disruption to production. The technical brief demanded highly controlled clinical conditions (protected from dust and vibration) for the manufacture of microprocessors, as well as conventional office space and a staff canteen.

The technical services run externally above a central 'street', supported by a steel framework from which the roof is suspended. This street is the heart of the scheme, linking the 'clean' (microchip production) and the 'dirty' (office and support) wings of the building. Above this street, an exoskeleton of masts provides support to services and to the two wings, allowing for column-free and extendable space.

Off-site fabrication allows for quick assembly, with a flexible system that allowed for the use of solid, opaque or transparent cladding panels.

Newport, Wales, 1982 – 7 (built)
Client: INMOS

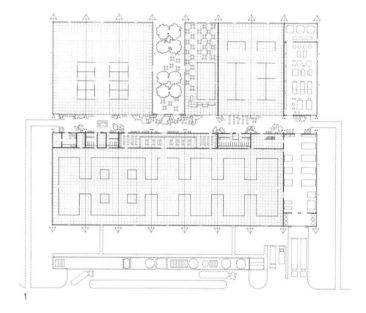

1

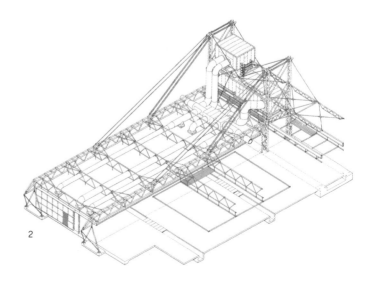

2

1 Layout plan.
2 Axonometric view.
3 Section showing how services are arranged along the central spine.
4 The building in its rural landscape.

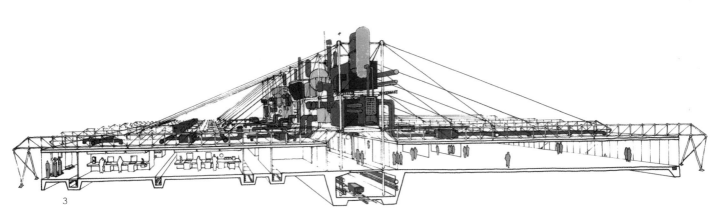

3

4

Mike Davies 'The concept drivers for INMOS were, as for the Pompidou Centre, large, column-free, flexible and universally serviced, open operational spaces. The heart of the scheme was a strong, central circulation spine and central meeting space for all employees.'

5

5 & 7   External structural details.

6   Flexible interior.

6

Michael Elias House

1

Los Angeles, USA, 1991 (unbuilt)
Client: Michael Elias

The steep hillside site, close to the Pacific Ocean, influenced the design of this house for a private client. The house stands in an elevated position, sunk into the terrain with its frontage emerging from the ground as a lightweight steel and glass pavilion.

The lightweight roof – twin steel masts supporting a floating roof plane measuring 18 × 27.5 m – floats over glass walls. Designed to be light and spacious, the living area uses frameless glazing to take maximum advantage of the views. To allow for future flexibility, internal walls were designed to be movable, constructed of prefabricated steel panels.

The house's setting within the hillside protects it from the climate, and supports a passive heating and ventilation strategy: heat stored in underground cavities is released to warm the house on cooler nights.

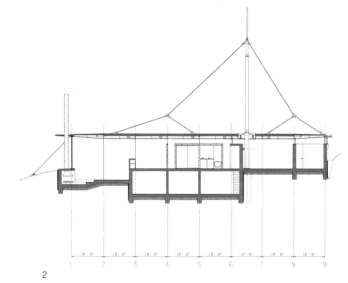

2

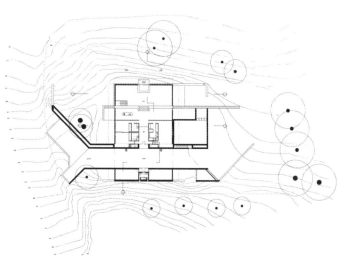

3

1 Concept sketch.
2 Section.
3 Ground floor plan.
4 & 5 Model, scale 1:100.

4

Designer Retail Outlet Centre

2

1 Roof canopy detail during construction.
2 Aerial view.
3 Concept sketch.

Ashford, UK, 1996 – 2000 (built)
Client: BAA McArthurGlen UK Ltd

This retail centre is located next to Ashford International railway station in Kent on a 30-acre former industrial site. Its tent structure unites the retail development creating a distinctive skyline which is clearly visible from the station and the surrounding flat landscape.

Rather than providing parking spaces around the outside of the retail centre as is the conventional solution, visitors' cars are contained within the centre of the development encouraging greater ease of access. All of the retail units are placed around the car park, united beneath an oval roof canopy creating shelter for pedestrians and uninterrupted views within the centre. The one-kilometre-long tensile fabric roof is the longest continuous membrane structure in the world and supported on only 24 bright orange steel masts.

Beneath the constant roof form, the retail units are self-contained and designed for ultimate flexibility, capable of undergoing rapid reconfiguration as tenants' demands change.

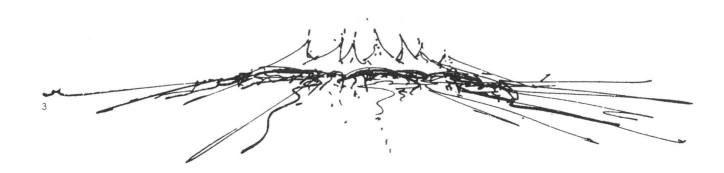

3

4 & 5 A curved circulation route for shoppers
connects all the retail units.
6 The retail centre at dusk.

Millennium Dome

The Millennium Dome was conceived as an iconic structure to celebrate the new millennium. It was the focus of a masterplan developed by the practice for the Greenwich Peninsula, a highly polluted and isolated former industrial site on the River Thames.

Offering flexible exhibition space across 100,000 m², the tent-like structure (formed of Teflon-coated fabric) is 320 m in diameter with a circumference of one kilometre and a maximum height of 50 m. Twelve outstretched towers – 100 m-high steel masts resembling arms outstretched in celebration – support the Dome and are held in place by more than 70 km of high-strength steel cable.

Key objectives of this project were lightness, economy and speed of construction, using standardised components. The Dome took just 15 months to construct and was delivered on time and on budget. It has now been remodelled as an entertainment complex, and forms one of the key venues for the London 2012 Olympic and Paralympic Games.

London, UK, 1996 – 9 (built)
Client: The New Millennium
Experience Company

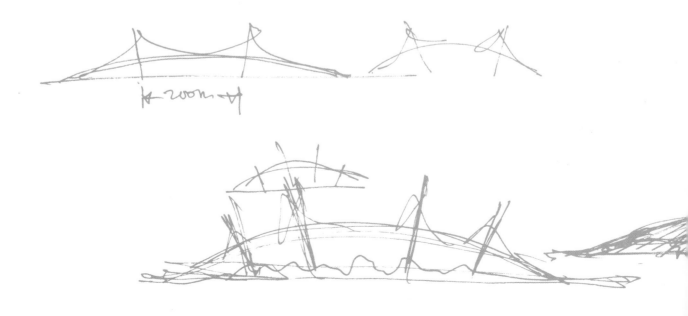

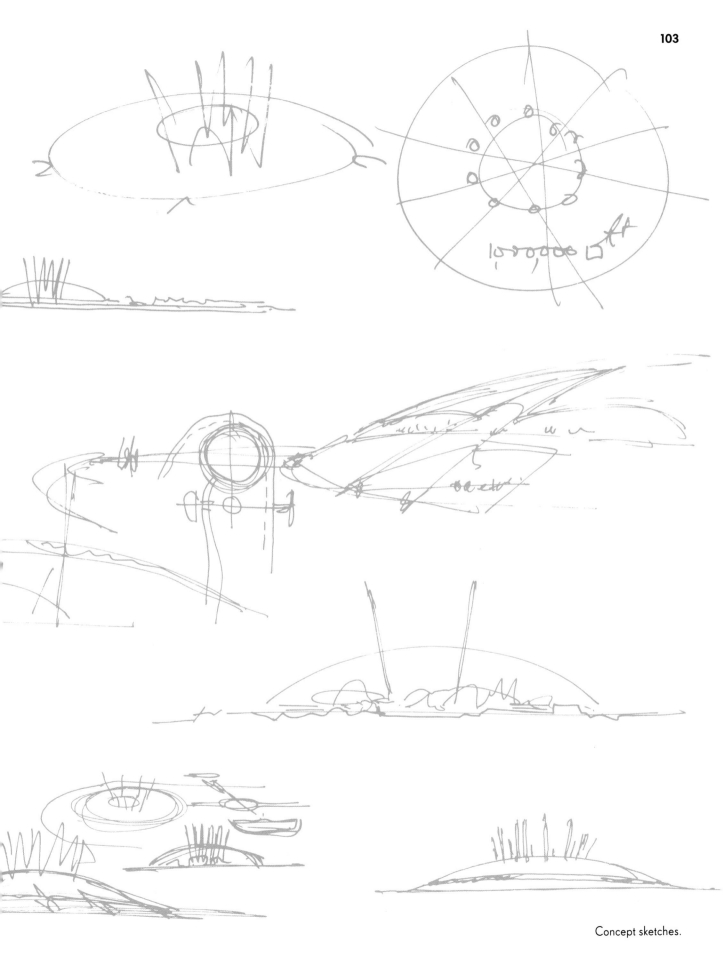

Concept sketches.

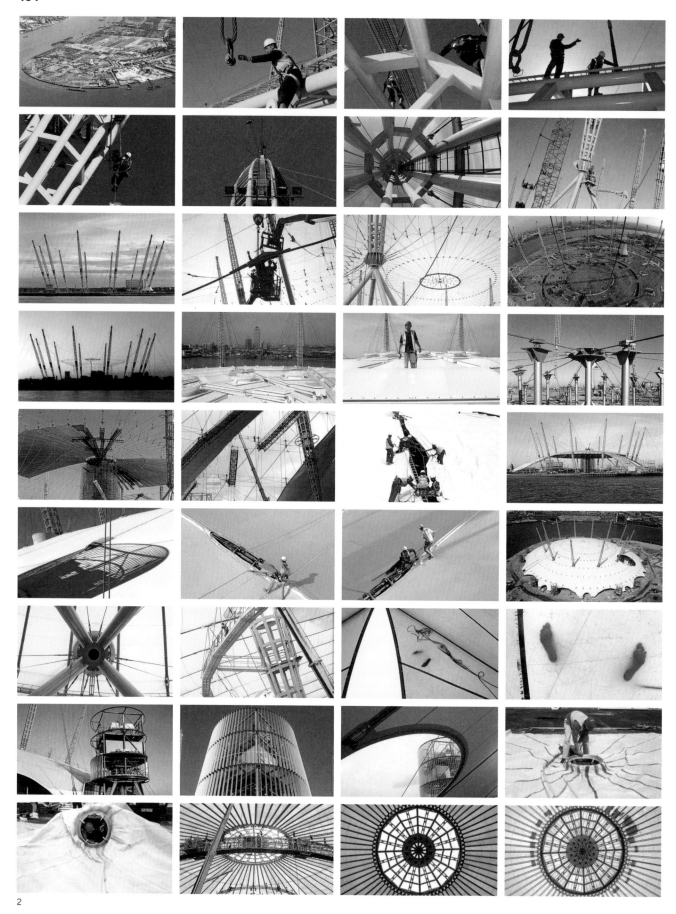

3

Mike Davies 'The ultimate inspiration for the Dome was a great sky, a cosmos under which all events take place – the radial lines and circles of the high-tensile roof structure recall the celestial reference grid of astronomical maps throughout the ages.'

2 Film stills of the Dome under construction.
3 Night-time views during events.
4 Aerial view showing relationship to River Thames and Canary Wharf.
5 Night-time view highlighting the Dome's structure (overleaf).

4

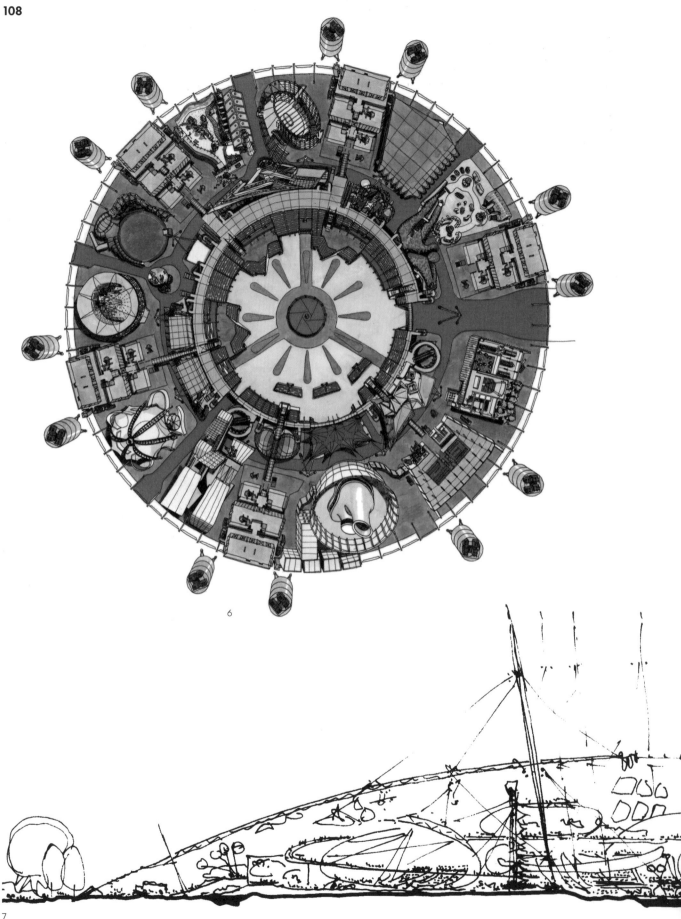

6

7

8

6 Interior plan showing exhibits.
7 Concept sketch.
8 Interior showing the central stage.

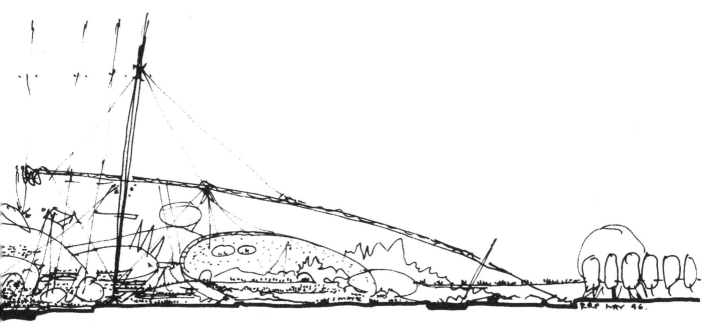

GRI

EEN

Global warming is the biggest single challenge threatening the future of the planet. The flow of CO_2 flooding the atmosphere – most of which comes from transport and buildings – must be curbed. Architects, scientists and politicians need to work together to reshape cities in such a way that ensures that they use less energy. Environmentally-benign processes, harnessing wind, water and solar power and the energy inherent in the earth itself, can do this.

The use of natural resources to warm and cool buildings provides the starting point for shaping our buildings and cities.

Bordeaux's Law Courts are both a response to a historic context and an environmentally-conscious design. Their glass skin reveals the courts within, but in the larger context of a global environmental crisis, the building's most radical characteristic is the use of passive systems of cooling and ventilation to minimise the use of carbon-generating energy.

In Cardiff, the National Assembly for Wales is another example of the marriage of democratic transparency to a progressive environmental agenda. The public space that surrounds the debating chamber is naturally ventilated and the ground on which the building stands acts as a cooling reservoir. The architecture responds to the social values that the building embodies, but it is also an example of a significant response to the crisis facing the planet.

ARAM Module

American doctor Lalla Iverson approached Piano + Rogers with a brief to produce a design for a standardised hospital unit which could be airlifted to developing countries in urgent need of medical services. The aim was to provide high quality medical facilities which would act as catalysts for regeneration in the communities which used them.

The resulting proposal was the flexible ARAM (Association for Rural Aid in Medicine) Module. The module consists of a 'hard' core, the technical equipment and services needed to diagnose and treat patients, and a flexible space for beds – normally no more than 200, though this figure could be reduced to 50 for isolated locations. The entire structure, made of small-scale, standardised parts, is designed to be transported and assembled by a non-specialist team.

Structurally, the module consists of latticed steel columns, with lightweight trusses supporting space decks suspended from high-tensile steel cables. The floor space of around 2,500 m^2 is interrupted only by the four main columns. Services are mounted in voids above and below the 'activity' floor, while power and other services are adaptable to suit local availability. Generating equipment and a crane for assembly are provided with the module.

1971 (unbuilt)
Client: Dr Lalla Iverson
Architect: Piano + Rogers

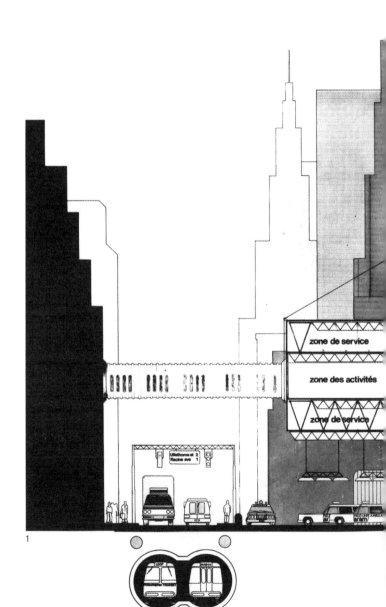

1

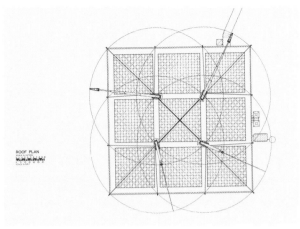

1 Concept drawing – section.
2 ARAM Module in rural context.
3 Roof plan.

ARAM Module in urban context.

Inland Revenue Headquarters

Nottingham, UK, 1992 (unbuilt)
Client: Inland Revenue

The scheme for this site, bounded by a river, a major railway line and a road, was designed to create buildings that are both environmentally efficient and sensitive to context, enhancing the setting of Nottingham Castle across the river.

The development, which comprises 40,000 m² of office space, is arranged in a great arc, facing a riverside park and looking over the river towards the city centre. The working spaces sweep down in two parallel blocks, separating public functions from private office areas, with landscaping between them.

Open windows provide natural ventilation, except on the southern façade bounding the railway, where an under-floor system supplies cool air. In the larger blocks, atria direct air to cooling towers which re-circulate warm air in the winter, and expel it in summer. Solar gain is controlled by tree planting between buildings and by screening devices on the façades. When artificial cooling is needed, the system is based on the use of groundwater rather than mechanical chillers.

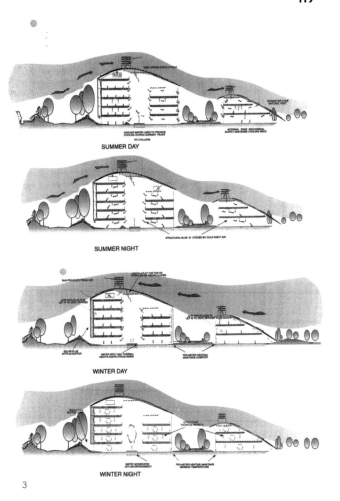

3

1 Model, scale 1:100 (page left).
2 Site section.
3 Strategies to develop a sustainable building.

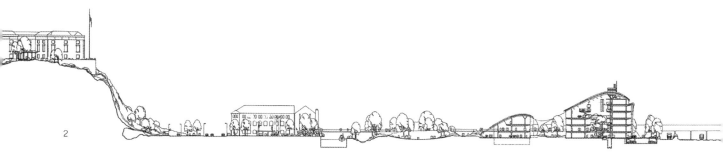

Turbine Tower

This research project – in conjunction with Ove Arup & Partners and Imperial College, London – developed from the practice's work on the Tomigaya Exhibition Building (see 'Legible'). It focuses on exploring a low-energy scheme for the Tomigaya site as a demonstration of the potential for environmentally-responsive building technology.

The design evolved from the premise that buildings should interact dynamically with the environment, taking advantage of free energy to provide comfortable living and working space. It researches the climatic and servicing requirements of a low-energy building.

Groundwater tanks are used to supplement the natural environmental controls of the building and a 'stack' effect extracts stale air. Reactive façades respond to extreme changes in weather conditions; an exposed concrete structure absorbs heat gain; water is used for cooling and wind for the generation of power. Exploiting the building's dynamic form, wind power produces 130 kW of energy per hour. The tower has the potential to be completely self-sufficient in energy terms.

The Turbine Tower marks a significant step in the practice's move towards natural servicing and the use of the environment as an 'architectural generator'.

Tokyo, Japan, 1992 – 3 (unbuilt)
Client: N/A

1

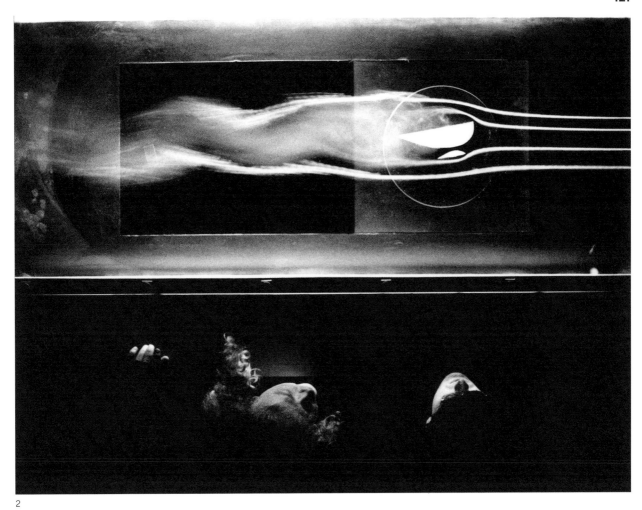

2

1 Concept sketch.
2 Wind tunnel testing to optimise form.
3 Model, scale 1:100.

3

Bordeaux Law Courts

1

2

3

Bordeaux, France, 1992 – 8 (built)
Client: Tribunal de Grande Instance

The Bordeaux Law Courts, designed while the European Court of Human Rights was being built, took the principle of balancing the public and private aspects of justice one step further by marrying it with an increasing focus on environmental efficiency.

The building has two distinct elements, oversailed by an undulating copper roof. The courts themselves face the medieval ramparts of Bordeaux and consist of seven enclosed flask-shaped wooden vessels set on stilts within public circulation space. Above this space, public access to the courts is provided from a raised walkway. On the other side of this atrium, a more conventional building provides judges' chambers and other 'back office' support.

The design takes a passive approach to heating and cooling. A heat sink cools or heats incoming air, which is distributed by low-speed fans and natural convection. Adjustable shutters and louvres regulate solar gain, and office windows can be opened to enable natural ventilation.

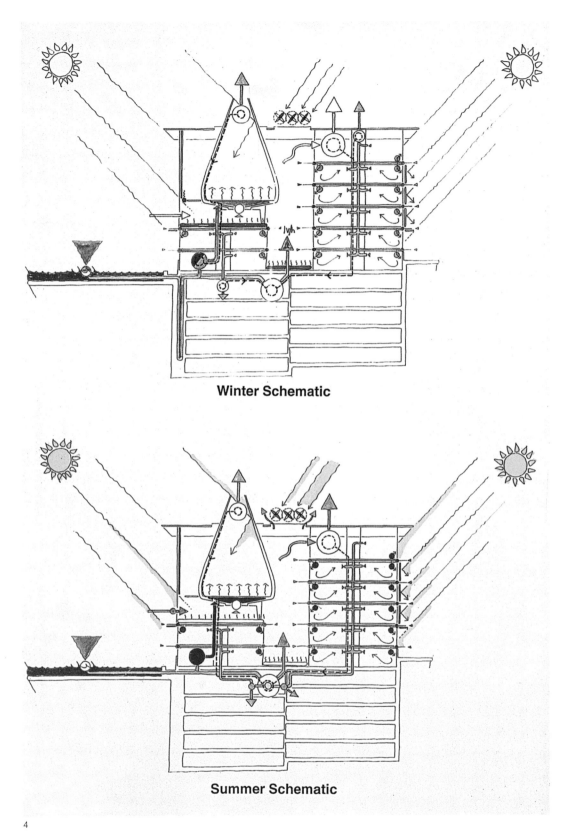

Winter Schematic

Summer Schematic

1 – 3 The design of the courtrooms takes its inspiration
        from traditional oast houses and boats.
4 Environmental concept for winter and summer.

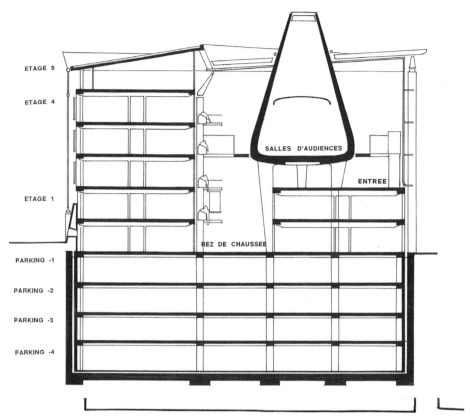

ETAGE 5
ETAGE 4
ETAGE 1

SALLES D'AUDIENCES

ENTREE

REZ DE CHAUSSEE

PARKING -1
PARKING -2
PARKING -3
PARKING -4

COUPE TRANSVERSALE TGI

5

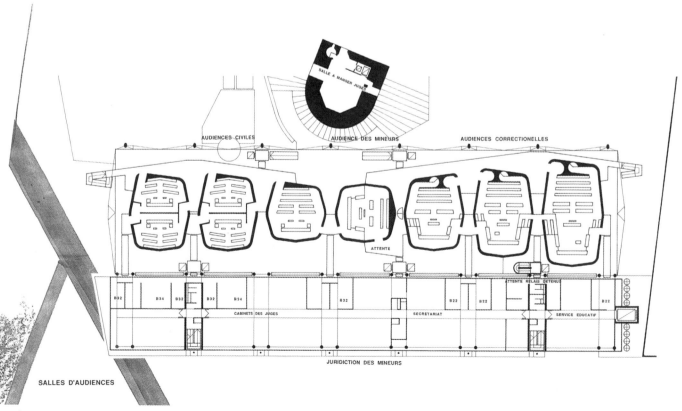

SALLE A MANGER JUGES

AUDIENCES CIVILES   AUDIENCE DES MINEURS   AUDIENCES CORRECTIONELLES

ATTENTE

ATTENTE RELAIS DETENUS

B32   B34 B32   B32   B34   B32   B22   B22   B22

CABINETS DES JUGES   SECRETARIAT   SERVICE EDUCATIF

JURIDICTION DES MINEURS

SALLES D'AUDIENCES

6

7

5 Principal cross section.
6 Plan.
7 Main entrance.

8

Amarjit Kalsi 'The key decision was to "liberate" the courtrooms from the "box". We had no preconceptions about construction and generated several concepts. The timber-clad solution was developed using a mix of high technology, computer-controlled machine work and traditional craftsmanship.'

8 Glass bridges link courts and administration areas.
9 Courtrooms above the Salle des Pas Perdus.
10 Public access to courts.
11 Courtroom interior.
12 Courtroom roof detail.
13 Night-time view (overleaf).

9

10

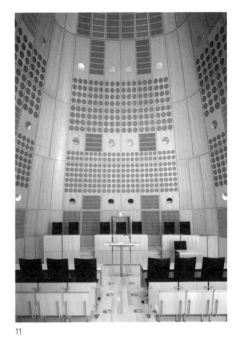

11

12

1964–7

Creek Vean, Feock, UK (built)

1967

Reliance Controls Electronics Factory, Swindon, UK (built)

1968–9

Rogers' House, London, UK (built)

1968–71

Zip-Up House (unbuilt)

don,

1982–5

PA Technology Laboratory, Princeton, USA (built)

1982–7

INMOS Microprocessor Factory, Newport, UK (built)

1986

London as it could be, London, UK (unbuilt)

1987–93

Kabuki-Cho, Tokyo, Japan (built)

built)

1994–7

South Bank Centre, London, UK (unbuilt)

1994–9

88 Wood Street, London, UK (built)

1995–2000

Lloyd's Register of Shipping, London, UK (built)

1995–2003

Minami Yamashiro Elementary School, Kyoto, Japan (built)

2001–8

Espacio, Madrid, n (unbuilt)

Maggie's London, London, UK (built)

2002

Sabadell Congress and Cultural Centre, Sabadell, Spain (unbuilt)

2002

Barcelona and L'Hospitalet Law Courts, Barcelona, Spain (unbuilt)

Centre for eville, Spain (built)

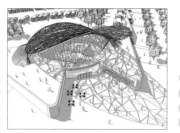

2006–

Metropolitana Linea 1 – Santa Maria del Pianto, Naples, Italy (ongoing)

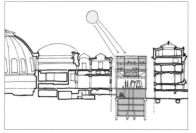

2006–

World Conservation and Exhibitions Centre, British Museum, London, UK (ongoing)

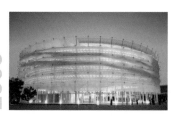

2006–

P7, Campus de la Justicia de Madrid, Madrid, Spain (ongoing)

60

Science Campus Project, Yale University, New Haven, USA (unbuilt)

Pill Creek Retreat, Feock, UK (built)

Fleetguard Factory, Quimper, France (built)

Coin Street, London, UK (unbuilt)

80

National Gallery Extension, London, UK (unbuilt)

Inland Revenue Headquarters, Nottingham, UK (unbuilt)

Turbine Tower, Toyko, Japan (unbuilt)

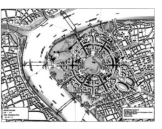

Shanghai Pudong Masterplan, Shanghai, China (unbuilt)

Bordeaux Law Courts, Bordeaux, France

00

Paddington Basin: Grand Union Building Scheme 1, London, UK (unbuilt)

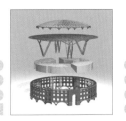

Las Arenas Bullring, Barcelona, Spain (under construction)

Canary Wharf, London, UK (ongoing)

Torr Spai

Ching Fu, Kaohsiung, Taiwan (built)

Barangaroo, Sydney, Australia (ongoing)

Design for Manufacture Housing, Milton Keynes, UK (under construction)

Palmas Altas Technology, S

Norman Foster, Richard Rogers and Carl Abbott

Standing: Tony Hunt and Frank Peacock
Seated: Aline Storry, Wendy Foster, Richard Rogers,
Su Rogers, Norman Foster and Maurice Philips

Richard Rogers, Su Rogers, John Doggart and John Young

Ruth Rogers, Peter Rice, Renzo Piano
and Richard Rogers

Renzo Piano and Richard Rogers

Roo, Richard and Ruth Rogers

John Young, Richard Rogers and Mike Davies

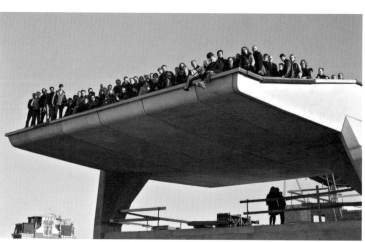

Site visit to Antwerp Low Courts

Standing: Marco Goldschmied, Su Rogers, John Young and Renzo Piano
Seated: Sally Appleby, Peter Flack, Richard Rogers and Jan Kaplicky

Pierre Boulez, Robert Bordaz, Richard Rogers and Renzo Piano

The Pompidou Centre team, Paris, 1972

John Young, Richard Rogers, Mike Davies and Marco Goldschmied

The team at INMOS

Graham Stirk, Laurie Abbott, Andrew Morris, Amarjit Kalsi, Mike Davies, Marco Goldschmied, Richard Rogers, Lennart Grut, John Young and Ivan Harbour

John Young, Mark Darbon, Richard Rogers, Mike Davies, Amarjit Kalsi, Lennart Grut, Richard Paul, Graham Stirk, Andrew Morris, Marco Goldschmied, Laurie Abbott and Ivan Harbour

Graham Stirk, Richard Rogers and Ivan Harbour

Graham Stirk, Lennart Grut, Richard Paul, Mike Davies, Richard Rogers, Andrew Morris, Ivan Harbour and Amarjit Kalsi

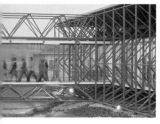

&B Italia Offices, Como, Italy (built)

UOP Factory, Tadworth, UK (built)

Lloyd's of London, London, UK (built)

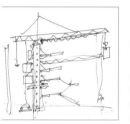

miagaya Exhibition Building, xyo, Japan (unbuilt)

Channel 4 Television Headquarters, London, UK (built)

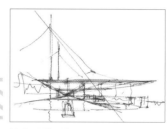

Michael Elias House, Los Angeles, USA (unbuilt)

Industrialised Housing System, South Korea (unbuilt)

Antwerp Law Courts, Antwerp, Belgium (built)

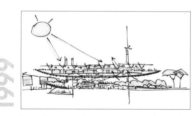

Rome Congress Centre, Rome, Italy (unbuilt)

National Assembly for Wales, Cardiff, UK (built)

on, Kaohsiung, Taiwan (built)

Bodegas Protos, Peñafiel, Spain (built)

One Hyde Park, London, UK (under construction)

Taipei, ng)

Far Glory, Taipei, Taiwan (ongoing)

Todawul – Saudi Stock Exchange, Riyadh, Saudi Arabia (unbuilt)

GyeongGi Do Provincial Government Offices, Seoul, South Korea (unbuilt)

Grand Hotel, Beirut, Lebanon (ongoing)

70

1971

ARAM (Association for Rural Aid in Medicine) Module (unbuilt)

1971–7

Pompidou Centre, Paris, France (built)

1972–3

B

1989–95

European Court of Human Rights, Strasbourg, France (built)

1989–2008

Terminal 5, Heathrow Airport, London, UK (built)

90

1990

Tokyo International Forum, Tokyo, Japan (unbuilt)

1990–2

Te
To

1996–9

Millennium Dome, London, UK (built)

1996–2000

Designer Retail Outlet Centre, Ashford, UK (built)

1997–2005

Terminal 4, Barajas Airport, Madrid, Spain (built)

2002–4

Mossbourne Community Academy, London, UK (built)

2002–

Parc1, Seoul, South Korea (under construction)

2002–

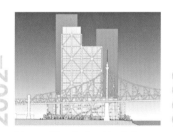

Silvercup West Studios, New York, USA (ongoing)

2002–

The Leadenhall Building, London, UK (ongoing)

2003–7

R9 Stat

2008–

Grand Paris, Paris, France (ongoing)

2006–

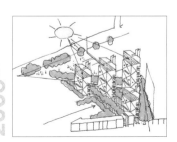

NEO Bankside, London, UK (under construction)

2008–

Centro Internacional, Bogotá, Colombia (ongoing)

2008–

Da-An Park, Taiwan (on

National Assembly for Wales

Looking towards the main entrance from the waterfront.

Cardiff, Wales, 1999 – 2005 (built)
Client: National Assembly for Wales

This building, on the water's edge at Cardiff Bay, creates a modern agora – a continuous public realm which steps up across the entire length of the site. This allows the public to observe the workings of the Welsh Assembly, while ensuring segregation and security as well as meeting the highest standards of accessibility and energy efficiency.

The raised ground floor – which sits beneath a floating roof – is separated from the outside spaces by a light glass wall. The most visible feature of the building is the funnel over the debating chamber itself, which is open to public view. Support services and committee rooms are set into the slate-clad plinth, enabling a segregation of public and private functions.

Virtually all areas of the building are naturally ventilated. A six-metre high, purpose-built rotating wind cowl provides ventilation to the debating chamber. Air conditioning has been eliminated from all offices and functional areas. A biomass boiler provides heating, while water usage is minimised by harvesting rainwater.

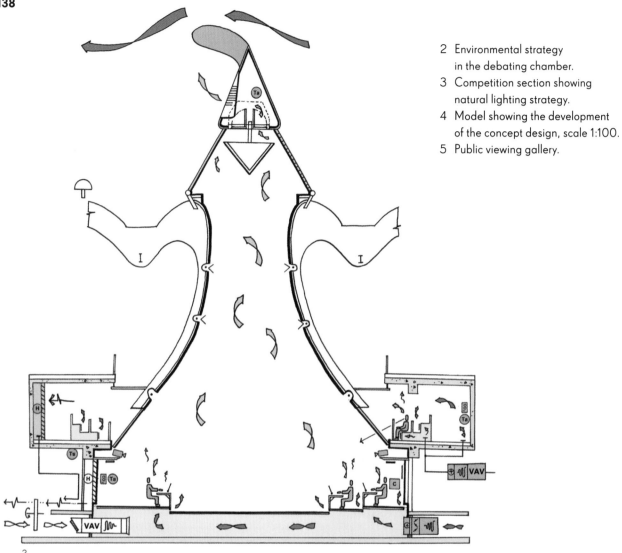

2 Environmental strategy
in the debating chamber.
3 Competition section showing
natural lighting strategy.
4 Model showing the development
of the concept design, scale 1:100.
5 Public viewing gallery.

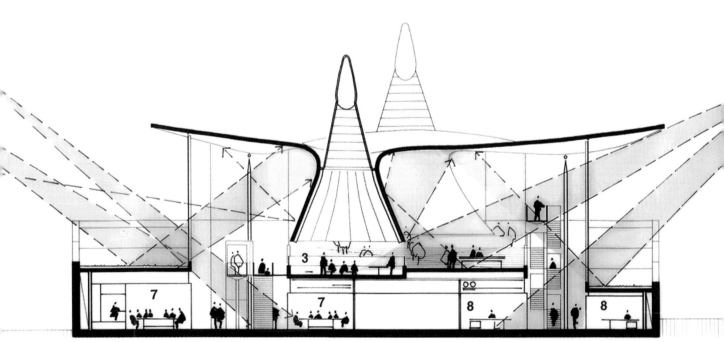

3

4

5

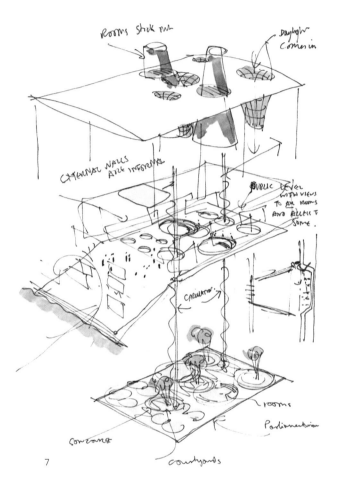

rooms stick out

Daylight comes in

external walls are informal

public level with views to all rooms and access t some.

circulation

rooms

Parliamentarian

concourse

courtyards

7

6 Debating chamber (left).
7 Exploded axonometric sketch.

Antwerp Law Courts

The Antwerp Law Courts provide 77,000 m² of space, including 36 separate courtrooms, creating a new landmark building to catalyse regeneration in the Bolivarplaats area to the south of the city centre.

The building is formed of eight narrow fingers extending from a central glazed space and connected by slender bridges. Wide steps, leading up from and continuing the line of Bolivarplaats, provide access to the Salle des Pas Perdus – a large glazed-roof central hall.

The wooden courtrooms sit on top of each spine, under soaring steel-clad roofs that allow views, daylight, shade and natural ventilation. Access is segregated for judges, defendants and the public.

The environmental strategy for the Law Courts is based on using the concrete frame of the building for night-time cooling, and on the reduction of solar gain by the use of high performance glazing and external, glazed louvres. The spinal structure of the building enables the use of natural lighting throughout, while natural ventilation is supplemented by low velocity ventilation for the hearing rooms.

Antwerp, Belgium, 1998 – 2005 (built)
Client: Regie der Gebouwen
Co-architect: VK Studio

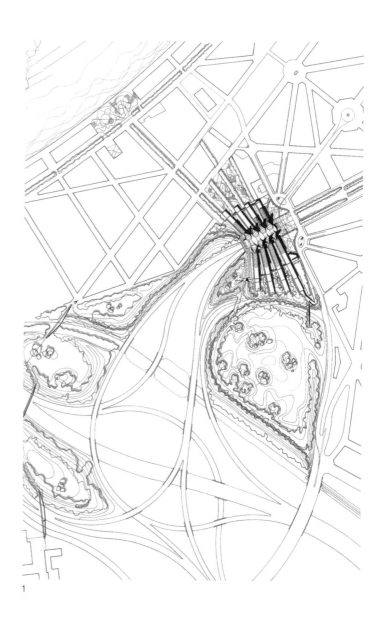

1

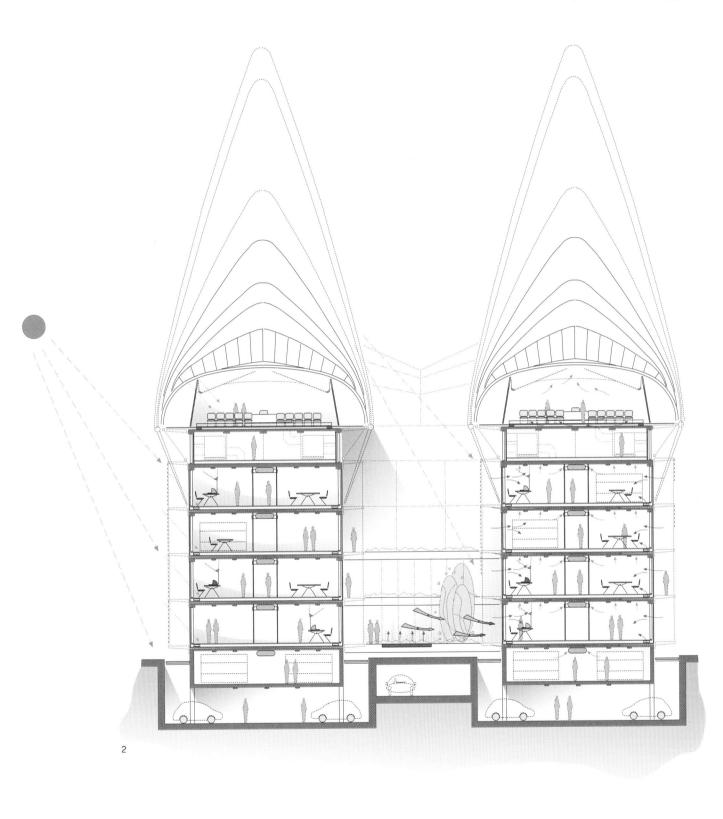

1 Competition plan.
2 Environmental cross section.

3

4

Ivan Harbour 'Despite the building's massive area, we wanted to create a structure that was sympathetic to the scale of the city. The result is a long, low building with a roofscape animated by the hearing room enclosures. We placed public spaces above the office areas so as to provide views across the city to the north.'

5

3 The Law Courts define the outskirts of Antwerp.
4 Entrance from Bolivarplaats.
5 Salle des Pas Perdus – interior view.
6 View of the large courtroom roofs (page right).

Mossbourne Community Academy

Mossbourne Community Academy represents a new approach to school design for a new type of school – a privately-sponsored state school for 900 pupils aged 11 – 16, in one of London's most deprived neighbourhoods.

The building responds to its difficult inner-city location by using its two wings to separate a focal courtyard opening up to the neighbouring green space from the busy railway lines that form the other two edges of the site. Each arm of the linear building is organised to create common vertical space and more traditional classroom 'decks'.

Regularly dispersed circulation and ventilation towers complete a framework that can be tailored to create separate 'houses' linked by a cloister facing the courtyard, or distinct floors for different subjects.

The building is an exemplar of low-energy design, from the sustainable timber frame structure to the ventilation systems. By opening windows, classrooms are naturally ventilated, and the six conical wind towers that rise above the building extract hot air from the internal atria.

London, UK, 2002 – 4 (built)
Client: Mossbourne Community Academy

1 Exterior view.
2 Concept sketch responding to site constraints.

1

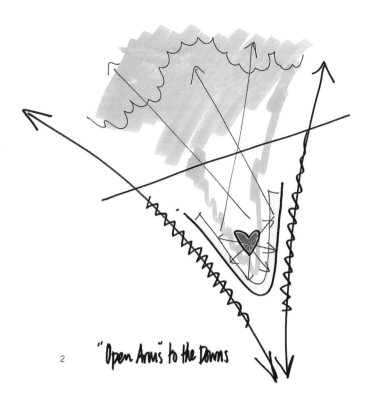

2 *"Open Arms to the Downs*

Ivan Harbour 'This project is all about putting pride back into a community. It is about ownership, equality and heart. It is about genuine approaches to sustainability through environmental design and material choices.'

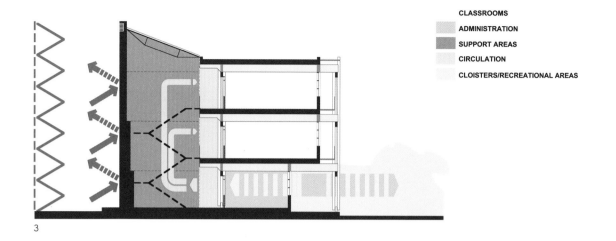

CLASSROOMS
ADMINISTRATION
SUPPORT AREAS
CIRCULATION
CLOISTERS/RECREATIONAL AREAS

3

5

3 Section showing teaching and support zones.
4 Exterior view showing double-height
   sports hall in yellow cladding (page left, below).
5 A top-lit computer resource space.

TRANSI

PARENT

Transparency in architecture is a representation of the breakdown of traditional hierarchies concealed behind masonry walls.

Layering materials allows for the play of light and shadow to be manipulated to create the impression of transparency.

A glazed façade can appear to be a blank mass by day. Light – both natural and artificial – serves to make a building transparent, as three office buildings in London demonstrate.

The atrium of the Channel 4 building is the hub of a busy media headquarters, naturally lit during the day, and transparent by night. 88 Wood Street's highly articulated façades are accentuated by the lights of the offices inside. Lloyd's Register of Shipping, in the City of London, also exemplifies transparency. Its towers project from a constricted site, enlivening the skyline and providing dramatic views for those who work inside.

Channel 4 Television Headquarters

The curved entrance is on a prominent corner site.

London, UK, 1990 – 4 (built)
Client: Channel 4 Television

Channel 4 was the UK's youngest broadcaster when it commissioned this scheme, to unite staff working in separate buildings and to express its identity as a dynamic, open, risk-taking organisation

As part of Rogers' courtyard masterplan, the building, which provides 15,000 m² of office space and some specialised broadcasting space, is located on two sides of a block, with a courtyard garden in the middle.

The building draws visitors into its concave glass-fronted lobby over a glass bridge that provides illumination for the rooms below. For passers-by, the striking suspended glass wall of the atrium provides transparency by day, and drama by night. The building is clad in aluminium and glass, with conference rooms to one side of the atrium, and services to the other.

Away from the street, the building curves out to provide space for restaurants and roof terraces, overlooking the central garden. A small square passes through the glass atrium wall between the reception area, the restaurant and the garden beyond, forming a transparent public zone linking the street with the garden.

3

John Young 'The key guiding principles for the design are reinforcing the existing pattern of this corner of Westminster, enclosing a public square at the heart of the scheme, and creating a striking headquarters building which is light, energy efficient, rationally organised and a pleasure to work in.'

2 The entrance showing lifts, stair towers and meeting rooms.
3 The curved glass wall is supported by a network of tension cables.
4 Interior of the entrance area.

4

5

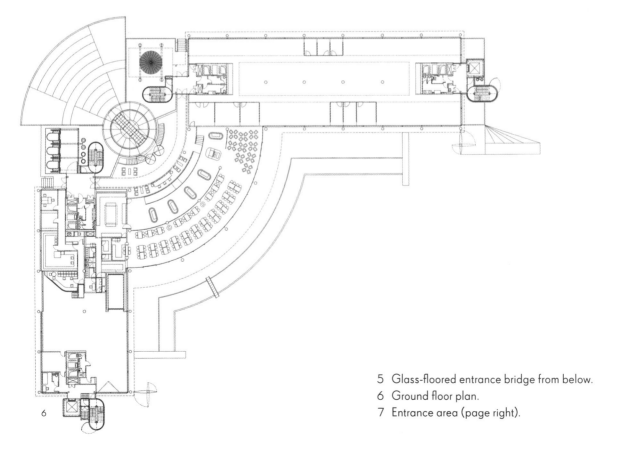

6

5 Glass-floored entrance bridge from below.
6 Ground floor plan.
7 Entrance area (page right).

88 Wood Street

88 Wood Street was originally designed as a landmark corporate headquarters for the Japanese bank Daiwa. Following the UK recession of the early 1990s, however, the brief changed to require more flexible and easily-lettable office space, and the building was entirely re-designed.

In order to make best use of a tight, irregular and architecturally sensitive site, the 33,000 m² building consists of three linked blocks that step up from 8, to 12, to 18 storeys, with service towers placed between them.

This structure enables light to permeate through the 'canyons' between the blocks. The façades of the main office floors are glazed from floor to ceiling, offering spectacular views of London. To minimise the need for electrical heating and cooling, the glass is triple-glazed and uses motorised blinds to respond to sunlight.

At ground level, the granite paving of the double-height reception area continues outside the building, breaking down the distinction between the building and the street, and blending 88 Wood Street into the historic grain of its surroundings.

London, UK, 1994 – 9 (built)
Client: Daiwa Europe Properties

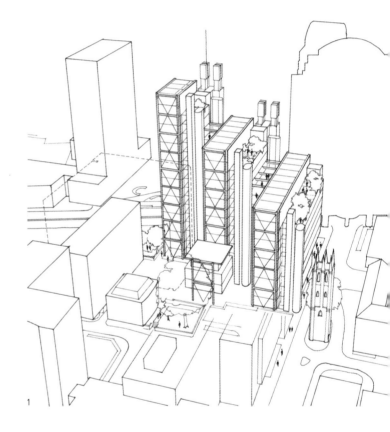

1

1 Aerial perspective.
2 Night-time view from London Wall (page right).

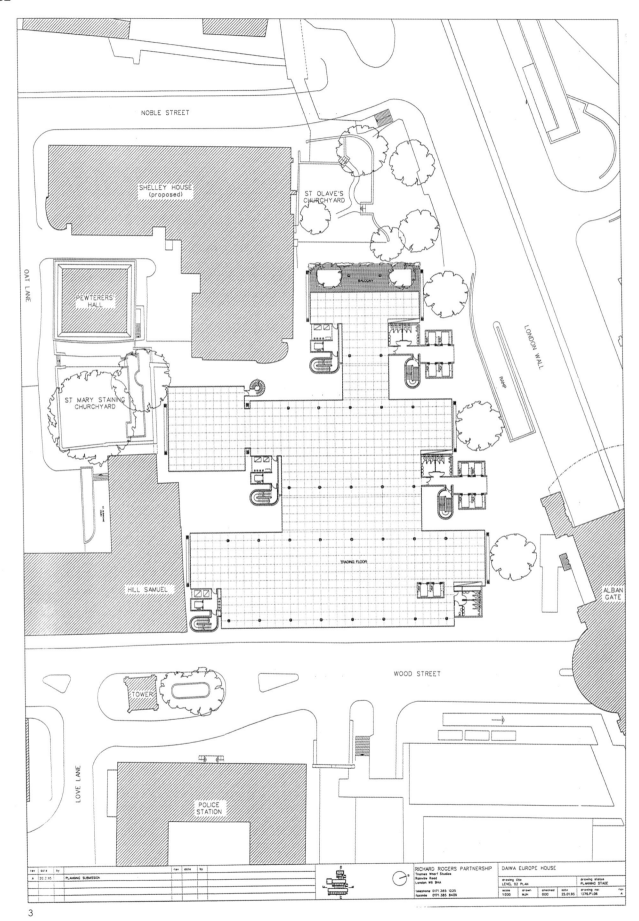

NOBLE STREET

SHELLEY HOUSE
(proposed)

ST OLAVE'S
CHURCHYARD

OAT LANE

PEWTERERS'
HALL

BALCONY

LONDON WALL

Ramp

ST MARY STAINING
CHURCHYARD

TRADING FLOOR

HILL SAMUEL

ALBAN
GATE

WOOD STREET

TOWER

LOVE LANE

POLICE
STATION

RICHARD ROGERS PARTNERSHIP
Thames Wharf Studios
Rainville Road
London W6 9HA

telephone 0171 385 1235
facsimile 0171 385 8409

DAIWA EUROPE HOUSE

drawing title
LEVEL 02 PLAN

drawing status
PLANNING STAGE

scale
1/200

drawn
MJH

checked
000

date
25.01.95

drawing no.
1376.PL06

rev
A

rev | date | by
A | 20.2.95 | PLANNING SUBMISSION

rev | date | by

4

5

3 Site plan.
4 Model, scale 1:100 showing stepped profile.
5 View of Wood Street frontage.

6

7

6 Interior of the double-height reception area.
7 Detail of stairs and lifts from the roof terrace.
8 Interior staircase.
9 Detail of lift interior.

Graham Stirk '88 Wood Street has been
designed to create a light, pleasant and
flexible working environment, incorporating
the latest advances in technology and energy
conservation. The key to this building is its
transparency. The vertical movement of people
animates the building, creating a dynamic
impact on the immediate surroundings.'

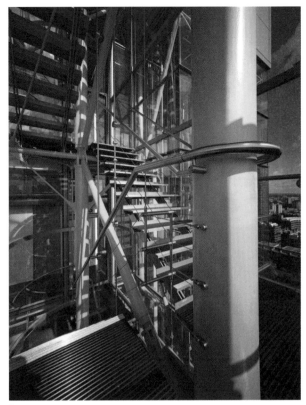

8

9

11

10 Night-time view from London Wall
(page left).
11 Detail showing lighting in lift cores.

Lloyd's Register of Shipping

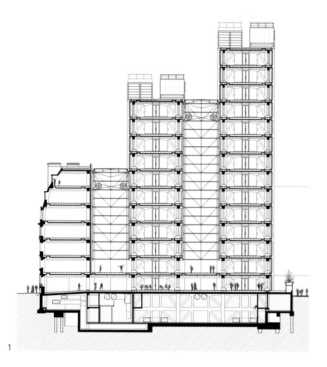

1

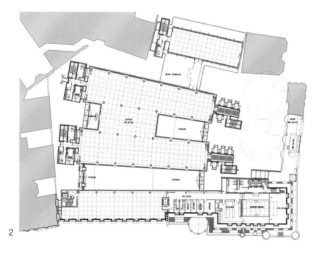

2

London, UK, 1995 – 2000 (built)
Client: Lloyd's Register of Shipping

The brief for Lloyd's Register of Shipping's London headquarters represented a major design challenge – to build new office space in a tight urban site, in the middle of an architecturally sensitive conservation area.

The building steps up from 6 – 14 storeys of office space with two basements, covering a total of 24,000 m². To respond to the shape of the site, which is defined by existing buildings on two sides, the building is structured around tapered floor-plates, creating a fan-shaped grid around two atrium spaces. These atria, and internal and external courtyards, allow daylight to penetrate the heart of the building.

Brightly coloured service towers with glazed lifts loom over the enhanced landscaping of the neighbouring churchyard. The glazed façade forms part of an integrated cooling and heating system, which enables the building to achieve a 33 % reduction in carbon dioxide emissions compared with conventional air conditioning.

1 Section.
2 Floor plan (4th floor).
3 View of the two central wings overlooking the courtyard (page right).

4

4 The two principal circulation cores
   from Fenchurch Street.
5 Elevation.
6 & 7 The entrance to the building is through
   a landscaped courtyard.
8 Glazed atria connect the office wings
   bringing natural light into the building.
9 Night-time view of a lift lobby (overleaf).

5

6

7

8

SYST

EMS

From the early days of the Modern Movement, the use of new building techniques to bring the benefits of mass production to architecture has been a recurring ambition. This ambition has finally become a reality. Innovative production processes and high-tech materials that were inconceivable two decades ago have made it possible for building systems to become flexible, adaptable and efficient. Architecture can now be the product of components made in the controlled conditions of the factory rather than on site. The discipline of such production methods gives form, scale, rhythm and legibility both to the individual parts and to the whole of a building.

The practice developed an industrialised housing system for a South Korean manufacturer based on prefabricated units stamped out of steel sheets, like cars. It can provide homes at a fifth of the cost of conventionally-built apartments.

Terminal 4 Barajas Airport, Madrid, is another example of the fusion of design and mass production. Visually, the terminal celebrates the poetry of travel. But the building's structure is based on a rational, repetitive building system driven by engineering needs. The result is dramatic but stems from a functional agenda rooted in the use of modern materials.

Terminal 5, Heathrow Airport

Some 30 million passengers annually will pass through Terminal 5, reinforcing Heathrow's position as the world's busiest international airport, which welcomes more than 70 million passengers a year.

T5 consists of a main terminal and two airside satellite buildings served by 56 aircraft stands. The main terminal is enclosed by a huge single-span curved roof, floating over the nearly 400 m-long departures hall, instilling a sense of calm over the intense activities below. Under this dynamic curve a vast day-lit public space houses check-in areas, retail spaces, restaurants, bars, passenger lounges, offices and baggage halls, all of which vary in size and height according to their function. An entirely free-standing internal structure allows long-term flexibility for all terminal activities. Behind huge sun-screened glazed façades, all vertical passenger movement takes place via the dramatic four-storey atria of the building.

Departing and arriving passengers cross a landscaped open piazza, or rise via high speed lifts from the rail station complex which connects Terminal 5 directly with central London.

London, UK, 1989 – 2008 (built)
Client: British Airports Authority (BAA)

1

1   Concept sketch.
2 & 3   Main terminal building.

2

3

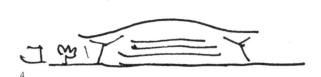

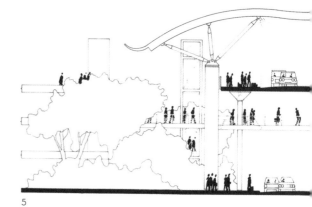

4 Sketches showing evolution of design.
5 Elevation (detail) – early design.
6 Sectional perspective – early design.

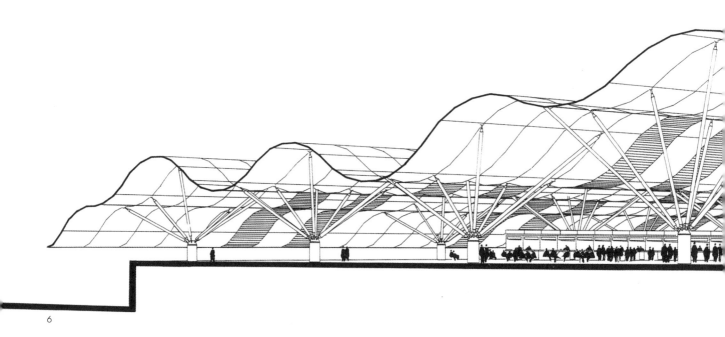

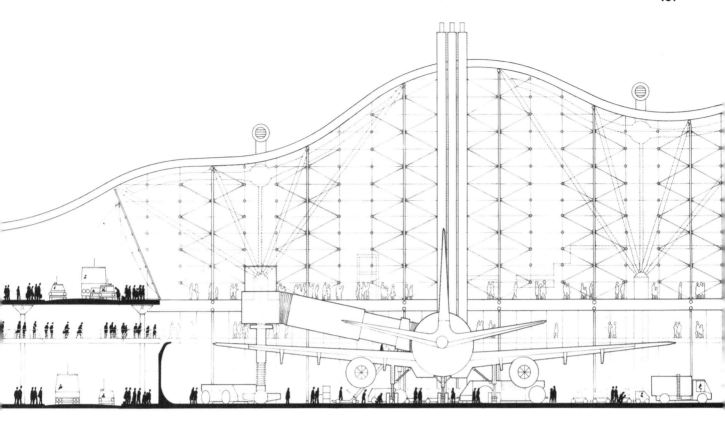

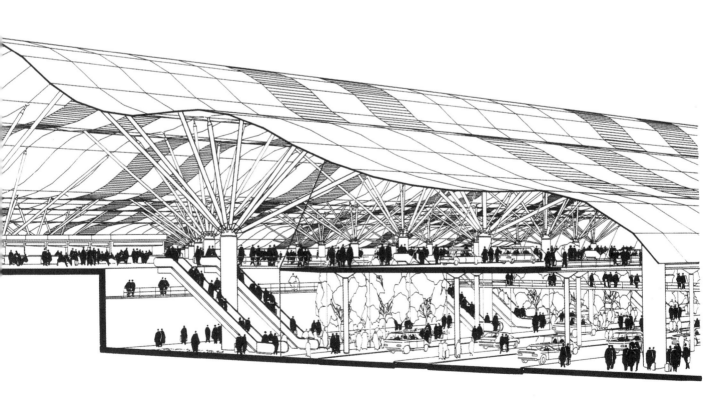

8

9

Mike Davies 'The project celebrates the magic of travel, creating a memorable place with a rich and varied public realm for travellers and those who serve them. Like London's great railway stations of the past, T5 has a civic role to play. Fulfilling the future demands of a world-class air terminal, it is designed to be a new gateway to Britain.'

7 Transport interchange piazza (page left).
8 Check-in area.
9 Waiting area and entrance
   to Underground station.

10

10 Detail of node.
11 Model, scale 1:2 of structural node on
    display at the Pompidou Centre, Paris.
12 Structural 'trees' at the edges of the
    terminal support the long-span roof.

11

Industrialised Housing System

Rapid urbanisation across the world requires new forms of housing which can quickly and flexibly accommodate growing populations, while providing the environmental responsibility and levels of comfort which the 21st century demands.

This design is for two-person homes, each measuring 43 m², at 20 % of the cost of conventional construction. The tiny units, including kitchens and storage space, can be pressed out of sheet steel in a factory, and assembled on-site.

The units are plugged in to a central core in a range of configurations, with minimal connection points. This allows for rapid on-site assembly using cranes, and enables different configurations – from towers to low-rise schemes – to respond to the varying landscape.

Core services include low-energy heating and cooling, as well as 'wired-in' communications, security and entertainment systems. Space is used as efficiently as possible, by designing furniture that can be pulled out or folded back for day-time and night-time uses.

South Korea, 1992 (unbuilt)
Client: Hanseem Corporation

1

1 Concept sketch.
2 Model, scale 1:100 of a high-rise configuration (page right).

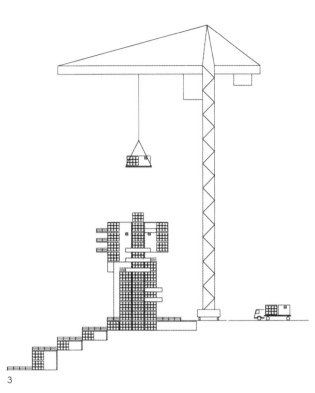

3

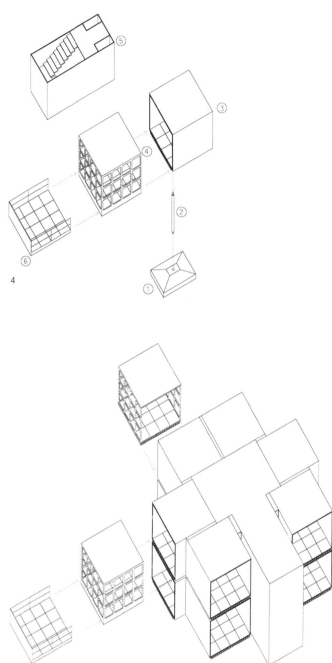

4

5

3 Elevation, showing units being craned into position on site.
4 & 5 Prefabricated kit of parts.
6 Modular kitchen assembly.
7 Plan showing alternative configurations of units (page right).

6

LEVELS 1-4

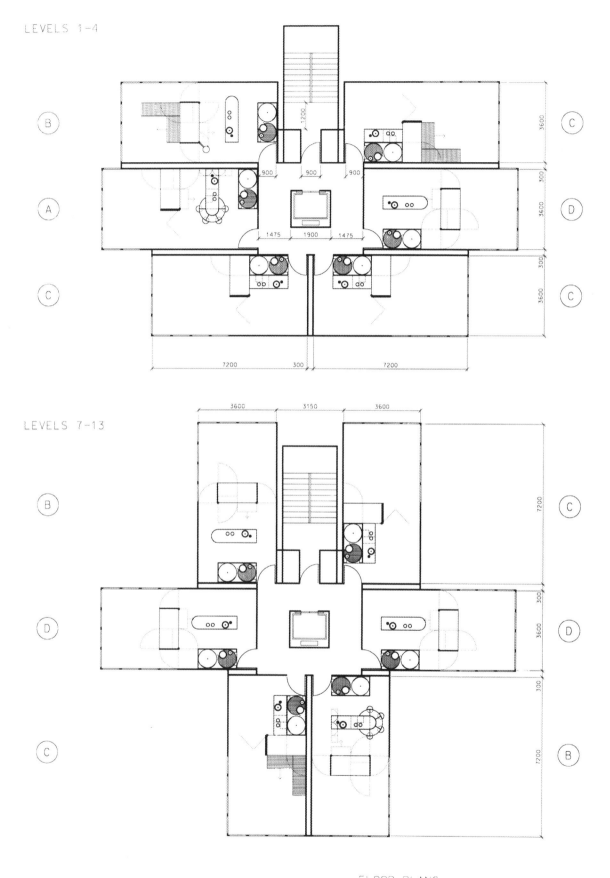

LEVELS 7-13

FLOOR PLANS

JUNE 1992

Terminal 4, Barajas Airport

Barajas Airport celebrates the excitement of travel and redefines the modern airport as a public space, a place for friends and strangers to meet.

The main terminal building is 1.2 km long and the project comprises more than 1,000,000 m² in total. Construction was completed in four years using a simple extruded form comprised of repetitive elements – concrete for the floor slabs and steel for the roof.

For a building of this size, a sense of scale and orientation is essential. The waves of the bamboo-lined roof create a sense of continuity and are supported by steel 'trees' of gradated colour, creating both joy and orientation. The terminal's openness, transparency and lack of corridors assist visitor orientation.

The building celebrates Madrid's quality of light with roof-lights allowing controlled daylight to flood the upper level. This natural light filters down into the lower levels through a series of parallel 'canyons', minimising the need for artificial lighting without exposing passengers to the fierce summer heat.

Madrid, Spain, 1997 – 2005 (built)
Client: AENA
Co-architect: Estudio Lamela

1

1 Aerial view of site showing terminal building during construction.
2 Satellite terminal showing main concourse (page right).

3

4

5

6

3 Aerial view showing the terminal and parking
   buildings under construction.
4 View of the south pier showing the gradated
   colour applied to the structural elements.
5 Airside departures gates and local control tower.
6 Aerial view of the departure gates.
7 Detail of the shading system.
8 Section through the airport (overleaf).

7

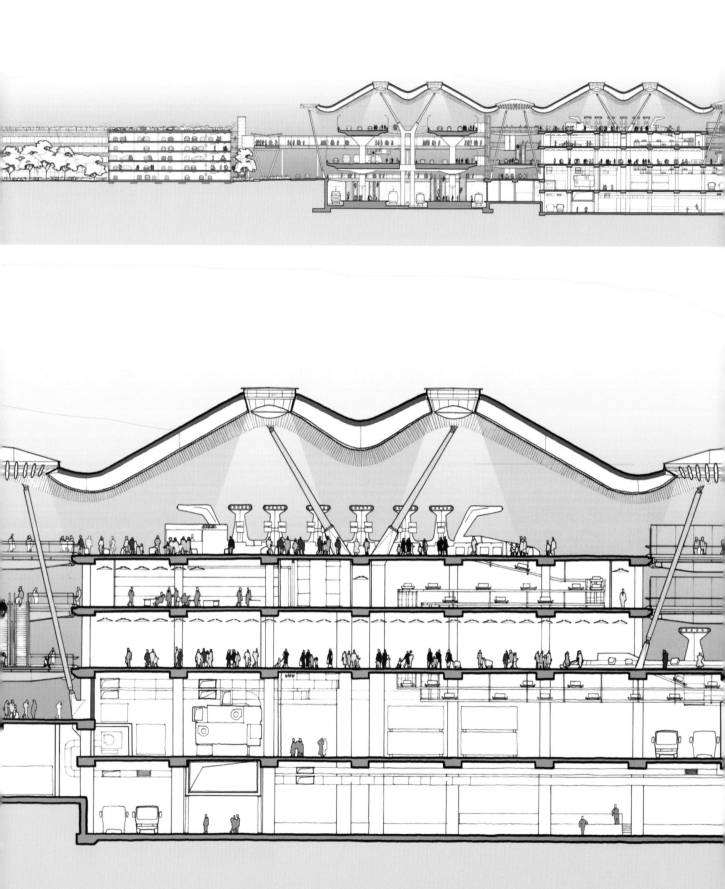

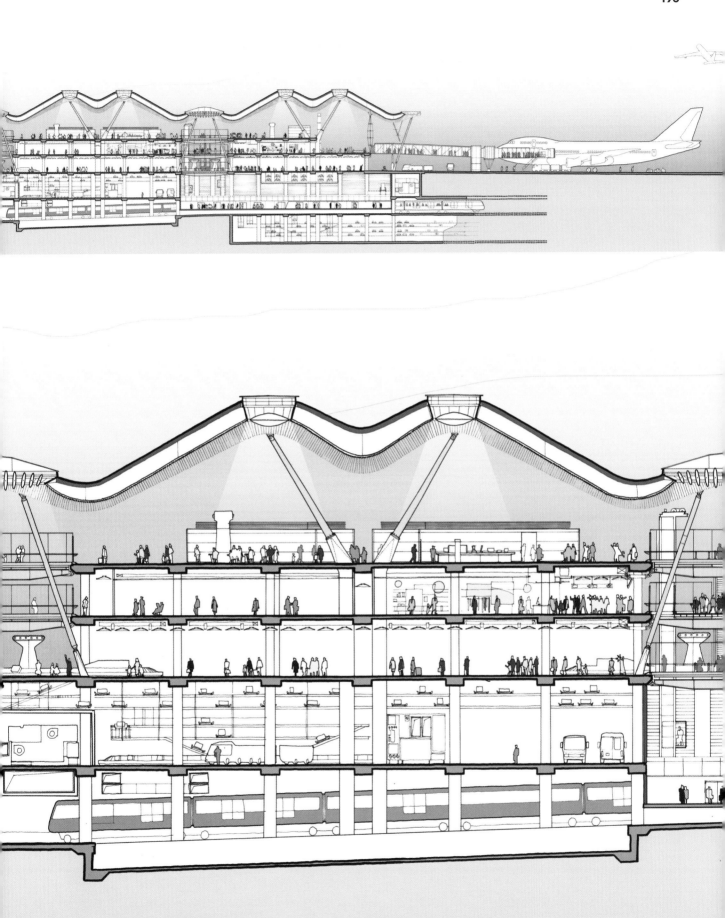

9

10

11

Richard Rogers 'Our aim has been to create an airport that is fun, with lots of light, great views and a high degree of clarity.'

9 & 10   Installation of the steel roof structure.
11   Detail of the steel structure at the roof edge.
12   Baggage reclaim area.
13 & 14   Natural light reaches all parts of the terminal building (page right and overleaf).

Bodegas Protos

Night-time view of the loading bay.

Peñafiel, Spain, 2003 – 8 (built)
Client: Bodegas Protos
Co-architect: Alonso Balaguer
and Arquitectos Asociados

This extension to a Ribera del Duero winery, consisting of a new building and a tunnel linking it to existing facilities, is a modern reinterpretation of traditional winery construction. An underground cellar maintains a constant temperature of 14 – 16°C and a production level above that is partly buried in the ground. The production and cellar levels also accommodate administrative and social facilities around a sunken patio.

The roof of the building is an articulated structure, generated by five inter-linked parabolic vaults of differing lengths. The roof form breaks down the overall mass and scale of the building to create a structure that is sympathetic to the surrounding urban grain and countryside.

Cool storage of the wine is created by effective use of the thermal mass of the ground and the exposed concrete structure. The south façade is protected by a nine-metre roof overhang while the east and west façades are shaded by a tubular rain screen. The terracotta tiles in the roof cover a ventilated cavity, allowing the sun's heat to be dissipated rather than radiating within the building.

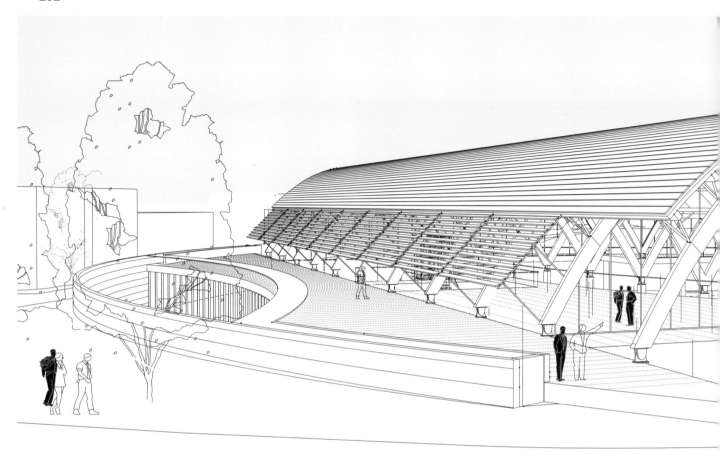

2

3

Graham Stirk 'A series of simple parabolic roofs create a form that is sensitive to the grain of the town.'

2 Drawing showing timber
roof structure.
3 View of winery under construction,
from the castle.
4 & 5 Concept sketches.

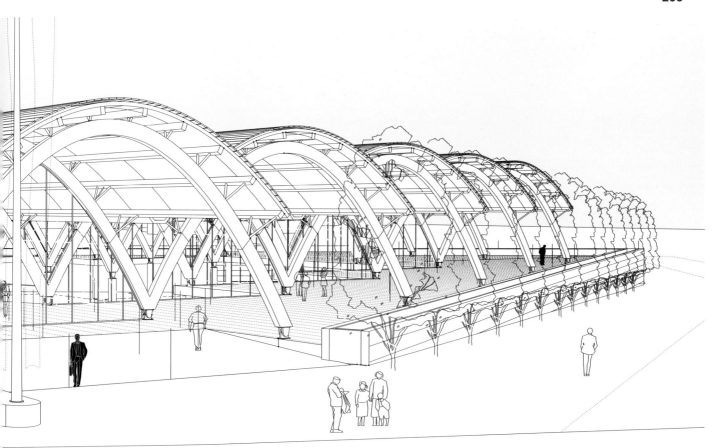

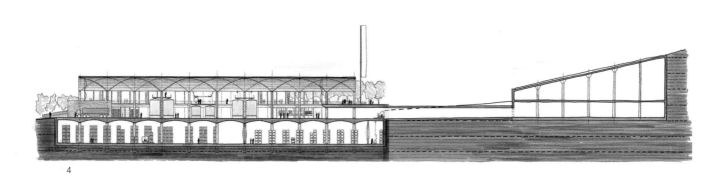

4

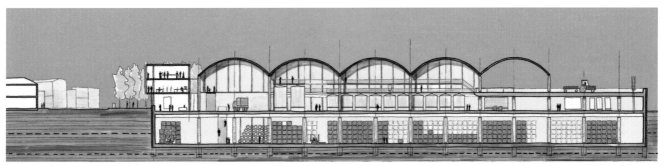

5

6 & 7 Sorting the grape harvest.
   8 Cleaning the tanks.
   9 Production level.
  10 View of the parabolic roof arches.
     (page right).

6

7

8

9

URB

BAN

Compact, multi-centred cities are the only environmentally sustainable form of urban development for future generations. They are a rational and economical way of creating human settlements that offer a high quality of life. They need to combine living and work, and encourage the rich and poor, the young and old to mix freely. Pedestrians, bicycles and public transport take priority over the car, and environmental responsibility is the driving force behind the planning of such settlements.

Rather than sprawling across precious countryside, cities need to utilise derelict land and empty buildings. The out-of-town shopping centre, the business park and the suburban housing development, serviced by the private car, are the enemies of successful cities.

Rogers' practice's masterplan for the Lu Jia Zui quarter of Shanghai, one of the fastest growing cities in the world, would have offered the chance of making of a truly sustainable, compact, 24-hour city, serviced by a comprehensive public transport system, with housing close to places of work. It was based on an urban grid that allowed for a variety of building heights and forms. It was a response to a competition staged by the city which, in the end, chose to opt for a different approach.

A similar approach has underpinned a series of urban masterplans for a wide range of cities, including Florence, Viareggio, Berlin, Manchester and London. In each case, compactness, sustainability and accessibility have shaped Rogers' strategy.

More than half of the world's population now lives in cities.

The only way to manage urban growth is by creating compact cities, driven by good design, social inclusion and environmental responsibility.

Architecture and urban design can transform the ordinary, giving order, scale and beauty to space.

URBAN STATEMENT

Increase Density

Density brings vitality to communities to make business prosper, and to make transport and other services viable.

Create Diversity

Compact cities mix people from all backgrounds, avoiding ghettos of privilege or poverty, and making citizens out of individuals.

Value Public Space

From park to pavement, public space provides a place for civic life, and for the meeting of people.

Re-use Land

Building only on previously developed land protects green space, prevents car-based sprawl and drives higher density.

Improve Transport

Make public transport, walking and cycling the most pleasurable and efficient means of transport.

Coin Street

1

London, UK, 1979 – 83 (unbuilt)
Client: Greycoat Estates

The Coin Street development proposed a substantial mixed-used development of offices, housing, leisure and retail along the River Thames. The aim was to bring new life to an area of the South Bank, which – at the time – had suffered a long period of decline.

The masterplan envisages a balance of public and private areas. A new glazed arcade connects Waterloo Station to the river and on to the City of London over a new footbridge. Pedestrian movement and public activities dominate at ground level, with office space and 300 residential units above and light industrial uses below. The proposals also include a new public space on the riverfront.

This scheme was proposed against an increasingly hostile and complex political and planning backdrop: there was strong pressure to protect views along the river, while the local community campaigned against office development. Nonetheless, Coin Street energised the debate on architecture and planning in the UK, and some of the masterplan's proposals have been incorporated into subsequent development on the site.

2

1   Model, scale 1:1000.
2 & 3   Public galleria connects South Bank
with City of London.

3

Richard Rogers 'The South Bank cultural centre opened up this key area to public access and is the most successful example of urban regeneration in post-war London. The Coin Street scheme was spearheaded by an exceptional developer – Stuart Lipton – and was intended as a complementary project, further revitalising this derelict area by providing a variety of public and private uses.'

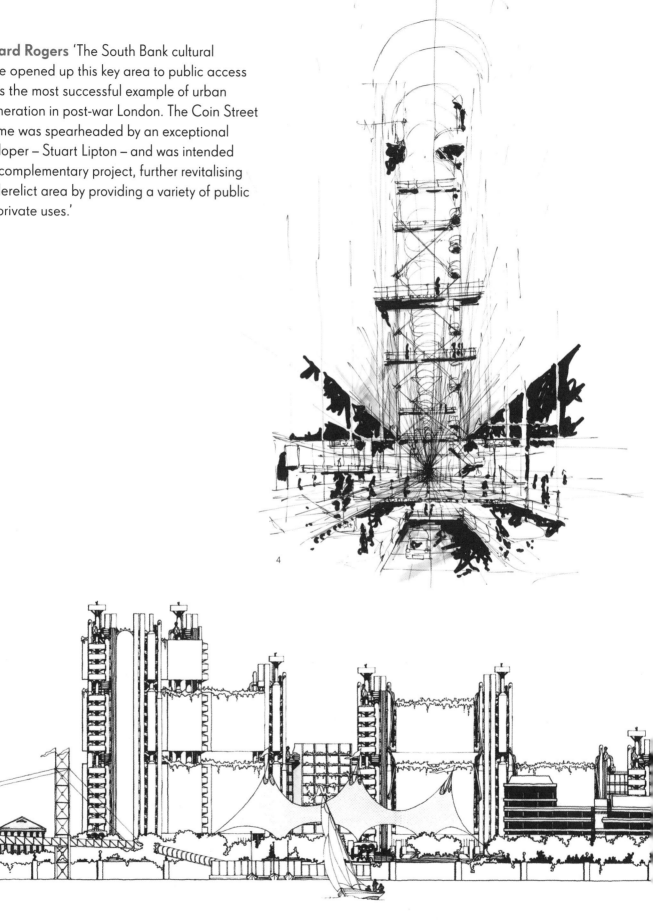

4

5

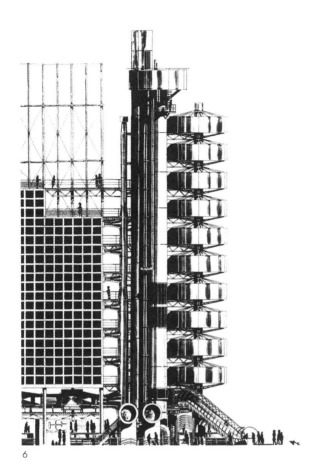

6

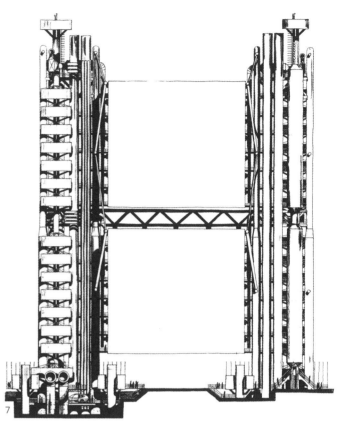

7

4 Sketch of galleria interior.
5 Elevation from River Thames.
6 & 7 Elevations showing structure and services

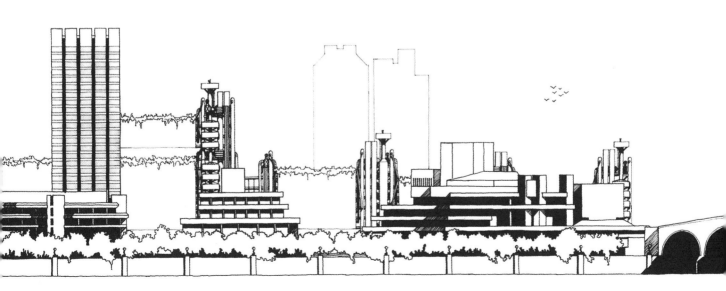

London as it could be

Richard Rogers 'At the heart of our urban strategy lies the concept that cities are for the meeting of friends and strangers in civilised public spaces surrounded by beautiful buildings.'

London, UK, 1986 (unbuilt)
Client: Royal Academy of Arts

Richard Rogers, Norman Foster and James Stirling, were invited to exhibit at the Royal Academy of Arts in London. Rogers took the opportunity to develop visionary – but workable – ideas for transforming a large area of central London.

Rogers' plan revolves on two axes: the Embankment along the River Thames from Westminster to Blackfriars, and the route across the Thames from Waterloo Station to Trafalgar Square – one of London's busiest squares. The proposal involves shutting part of Trafalgar Square to traffic and sinking the road that runs along the Embankment into a tunnel, allowing the riverside to become a new linear park.

Moving Charing Cross Station south of the river allows a lightweight pedestrian bridge to replace the bulky Hungerford railway bridge. Floating islands with restaurants and shops connect to this bridge, allowing the Thames to become a focus for activity rather than a sterile gulf between North and South London. The concept has formed part of today's pedestrian-based strategy for this part of London.

Sinking the road creates a new public realm.

2

3

2 & 5 Sketches showing free pedestrian movement in front of the National Gallery / Trafalgar Square.

3 & 4 Traffic congestion in Trafalgar Square.

4

5

6

7

8

6 Plan showing the two principal
  areas of pedestrian movement.
7 Sketch showing public amenity
  island and bridge.
8 Sketch showing bridge with
  cross-river shuttle.
9 & 10 Model, scale 1:100, of proposed
  bridge and amenity island.

9

10

Shanghai Pudong Masterplan

1 Final massing model, scale 1:2000.
2 Animated model, scale 1:2000, used in 'Richard Rogers
   + Architects: From the House to the City' exhibition.
3 Model, scale 1:1000 to show density and mix of use.

At the tip of the Pudong Peninsula, the Lu Jia Zui area was cut off from the city centre by the Yangtze River. The practice was invited by the city authorities to propose ideas for major development in an area supporting 800,000 people.

The response applies the principles of a sustainable compact city, to create 'a diverse commercial and residential quarter enhanced by a network of parks and public spaces.' A park forms the core of the district, with boulevards radiating outwards, and public transport nodes forming a ring around it.

These light rail nodes are linked to new pedestrian and cycle routes, and are the driver of urban form: higher density high-rise development is clustered around these nodes to form six neighbourhoods. Commercial and residential areas are located within walking distance of each other and are also close to other infrastructure.

Underpinning the masterplan is attention to environmental efficiency at the level of the urban district, as well as individual buildings – the energy programme aimed at reducing consumption by 70 % compared with a conventional development of the time.

Shanghai (Pudong), China, 1992 – 4 (unbuilt)
Client: Shanghai Development Corporation

2

3

KEY

Existing or planned items are listed in black
Additional infrastructure advised is shown in red

Primary Roads	
Tunnel	
Distribution Roads	
Metro	
Metro additional	
LRT	Station/Parking
Tram	Stop
Ferry	
Cable Cars	

SHANGHAI - PU DONG - 1992

RICHARD ROGERS PARTNERSHIP
Ove Arup and Partners

PLAN SHOWING PLANNED AND PROPOSED
TRANSPORT INFRASTRUCTURE

Scale 1:5000   January 1993

4

4 & 5 Transport strategy creating an overlapping
system of separate but interrelated networks.

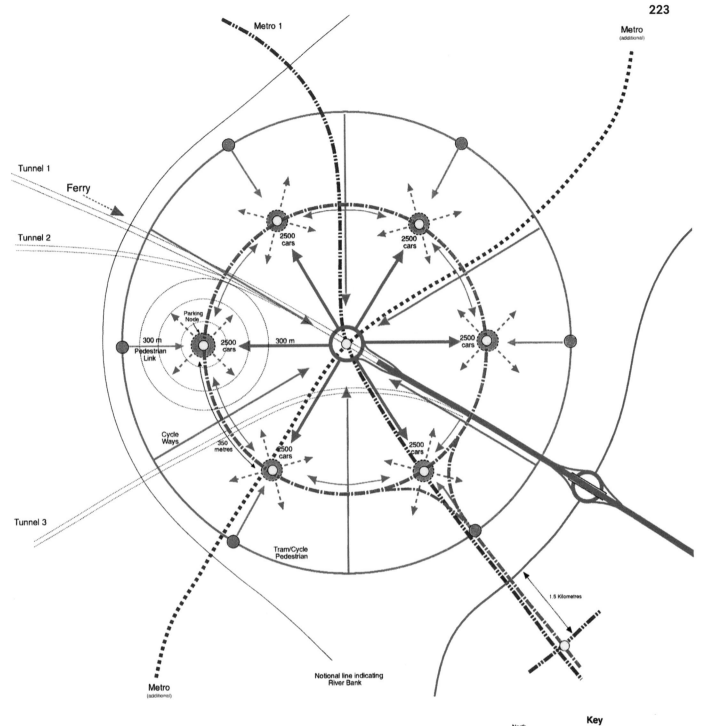

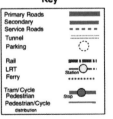

Graph Showing Comparative Energy Use for Lu Jia Zui

These estimates are based on a total of 5.3 million square metres, 50% of which is office accommodation

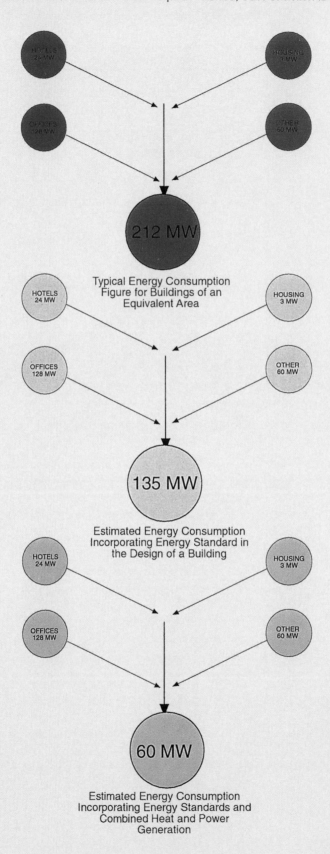

Typical Energy Consumption Figure for Buildings of an Equivalent Area

Estimated Energy Consumption Incorporating Energy Standard in the Design of a Building

Estimated Energy Consumption Incorporating Energy Standards and Combined Heat and Power Generation

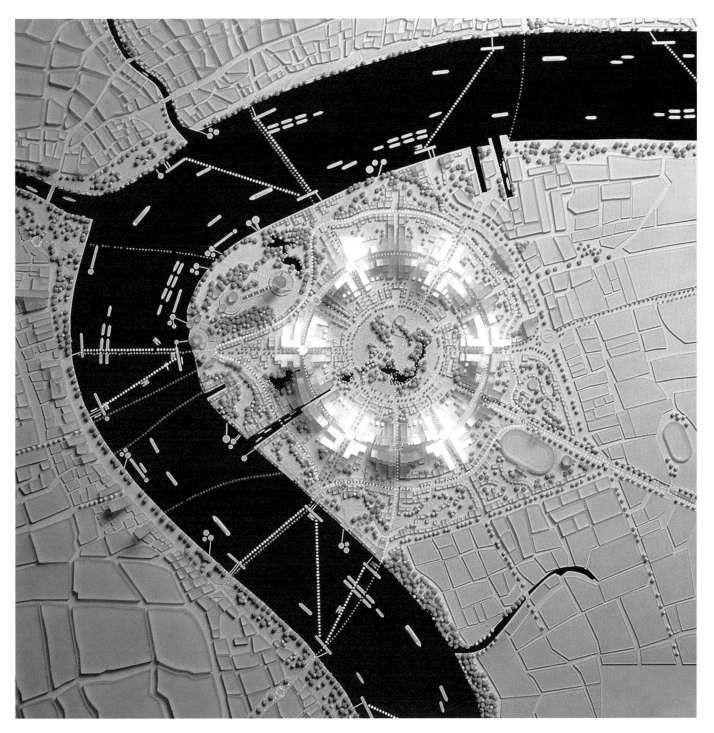

6 Comparative energy use.
7 Transport links into the proposed
  new urban district (this page).

Richard Rogers 'Our scheme offered the
possibility of a truly sustainable, compact,
24-hour city.'

I am passionate about cities. They are the very drivers of our culture and of our economy. The only sustainable form of development in the modern age is the compact, well-connected, well-designed, environmentally-responsible, live-work-leisure city, where poor and rich can co-exist side by side and not in ghettos.

Cities are first and foremost for the meeting of people – for friends and strangers, and for the exchange of goods and ideas. The concepts of citizenship, civil society and civic responsibility were all born in the city. Interesting things can happen when there is a mix of people and activities in flexible spaces. Well-designed buildings and public spaces can encourage social inclusion and bring joy to users. If we build well, we can create a socially inclusive environment.

A way of measuring the quality of life in cities is by the design of public spaces which can contribute great vitality. Every individual should have the right to well-designed public space – this should be part of a charter of human rights. Everybody should be able to sit on their own door step or a bench close to their home, and they should be able to see a tree from their window. Everyone should be able to find a public square a few minutes from their front door and be able to reach a park easily.

The most important rule of successful sustainable urban development is to develop only brownfield land and underused buildings and not to expand onto greenfield sites. Rather, we should build a hypothetical 'wall' around the existing city or, better still, a green belt, and use this to encourage denser development around public transport hubs. Intensification of existing land allows existing facilities – such as transport, schools, hospitals, government buildings, as well as roads and

public transport – to be used, thereby limiting the use of cars and discouraging suburban sprawl.

Information technology has given us the power to study and analyse the global power of cities. If you look at satellite pictures of the earth at night, you can see a clearly defined and far-reaching network of cities in many parts of the world. Today, more than 50 % of the world's inhabitants live in cities, whereas 100 years ago it was only 10 %. We need to ensure that modern cities are designed on a scale which is relevant to the needs of the citizens who inhabit them and which encourage people to walk around and meet in a safe environment where individuals are literally the 'eyes and ears' on the street.

The biggest crisis we are all facing is climate change. If we do not make clear decisions about the control of carbon fuels, we could witness the destruction of mankind in the foreseeable future. Buildings and transport are responsible for around 70 % of all CO_2 in the world and architecture – including city planning – can have a major impact on reducing these emissions. Depending on how we plan, we can make some big improvements. All energy ultimately comes from the sun, and we need to harness clean energy using climate-friendly technology that does not produce CO_2, by using not only the sun itself but also the wind, the sea and thermal energy. We have to see the earth as a living, organic entity that we must respect – and that we are responsible for. Global warming as well as our dependence on carbon-based fuel needs to be reduced quickly and dramatically. Climate change is happening all around us. If it continues at its current rate, it will not only destroy the glaciers of the Arctic and Antarctic regions, it will also destroy mankind. We are already witnessing the effects of climate change in terms of flooding, famine and political extremism.

Teamwork is the key to good urban design. A project is not the work of a single person; it is made by many talented partners, great clients, good construction teams and consultants all working together. As a practice, we are interested in the social environment and social inclusion as well as the beauty of the environment in which we live and work. As architects, we give order, scale and rhythm to space, in a celebration of beauty and function, of science and art.

Richard Rogers

S AND
JTURE

WOR
PROG

WORK IN PROGRESS

Current and future works are featured in this section which demonstrates how Rogers' approach is evolving as a result of the influence of his younger partners, Graham Stirk and Ivan Harbour. Within this section, the themes that define the partnership's work have been adapted to make them relevant to new global demands and requirements, including shifting attitudes towards the live-work balance and greater awareness of environmental issues – particularly the impact of climate change on the planet. This section also underlines the truly international nature of Rogers' practice, which is already working on projects in four continents and continually adapting its design philosophy to meet new challenges in new locations. It demonstrates that the fundamental principles of architecture can still be clearly seen through innovation.

The Leadenhall Building

This 50-storey tower rises to a height of more than 220 m and will become a landmark on the London skyline.

The building's tapering profile is prompted by a requirement to respect views of the nearby St Paul's Cathedral. The floorplates of the fully glazed office floors progressively diminish in depth towards the apex of the building.

Instead of a traditional central core, the design employs a 'mega-frame' structure, which also defines the perimeter of the building. The circulation and servicing core is located in a north-facing peninsular tower, with recesses cut between this tower and the main tower to maximise natural lighting.

Although the building occupies the entire site, the scheme delivers an unprecedented allocation of public space – the lowest seven levels are removed to provide a sun-lit public realm, with shops, exhibition space, soft landscaping and trees. This new public space will provide a rare oasis within the dense urban character of the City of London.

London, UK, 2002 – (ongoing)
Client: British Land

1

1 View of the north core.
2 Perspective showing building in context.

2

Canary Wharf

Canary Wharf's success has been achieved through the development vision of the Canary Wharf Group. Steady housing growth and the emergence of Canary Wharf as an international business district has brought about the economic revival of London's Docklands area.

Rogers Stirk Harbour + Partners is designing two schemes with Canary Wharf Group, and a third with the Wood Wharf Partnership (WWP), a partnership between Canary Wharf Group, British Waterways and Ballymore Properties. The Wood Wharf masterplan is a new inner-city mixed sustainable development, which will revitalise a seven-hectare, part-brownfield site adjacent to Canary Wharf. The project will provide homes around a significant commercial heart, creating substantial employment, a new park, public waterside spaces and community facilities.

The other two schemes are for office complexes in the area – Riverside South and Heron Quays West – for the international business market on spectacular river and dockside locations. Both projects provide market standards of financial trading accommodation, creating facilities that will contribute to London's reputation as a centre for world finance.

London, UK, 2000 – (ongoing)
Client: Canary Wharf Group

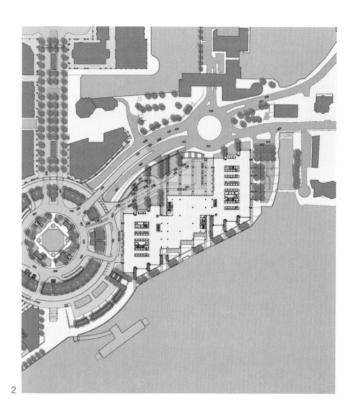

2

3

1   Aerial view of proposed Riverside South scheme (page left).
2   Ground floor plan of Riverside South scheme.
3   Riverside South scheme building in context.

R9 Station

On the new 'Red' line of Kaohsiung's underground system, the R9 station is designed to serve the city's Central Park and an adjacent shopping district.

The design draws the landscaping down from the park into the station concourse – via the main entrance – some 11 m below ground level. Two sets of escalators – divided by a cascading water feature – link the concourse and park levels. A large aluminium canopy – measuring 50 m x 50 m in the shape of a concave trapezoid and sitting on four yellow steel 'trees' – oversails the entire concourse area, protecting it from strong sunlight and rainfall. Aluminium was chosen due to its lightness, durability and resistance to corrosion. Across the canopy's top surface are a large number of glazed openings filled with frosted glass. On the underside, these openings are perforated to allow natural light to penetrate to the concourse below while also helping to dissipate the sun's glare. Interior walls are covered by prefabricated mosaic panels, while the ceiling comprises perforated aluminium panels backed by sound absorbent fabric. As well as the main entrance, RSHP has also designed two sub entrances to the station with their own distinctive aluminium canopies supported on smaller yellow steel 'trees'.

Kaohsiung, Taiwan, 2003 – 7 (built)
Client: Kaohsiung Rapid Transit Corporation

STATION AS VIBRANT MEETING PLACE
1

FOCUS ON THE TICKET HALL

2

1 & 2 Concept sketches.
3 & 4 Views of the canopy.

3

4

One Hyde Park

One Hyde Park occupies one of London's prime sites. The form of the development has been driven by spectacular views to the north across the park, as well as by the need to respect the neighbouring historic buildings in Knightsbridge. In order to maximise views, the design proposes four pavilions separated by transparent stairs and lift cores, The pavilions step up from 10 – 14 storeys, each set on a double-height 'podium' along Knightsbridge, providing scale, grain and legibility to the overall development.

This scheme delivers 80 flexible residential luxury apartments and duplexes, including four penthouse suites. The design also incorporates reception facilities for the residential component of the scheme, and three retail units at ground-floor level. In total, the development offers 35,340 m^2 of residential and 1,200 m^2 of retail.

The scheme aims to minimise the environmental impact of the building and its engineering systems, and to reduce carbon emissions. It incorporates geothermal wells, which use ground water for heating and cooling, and a system for rainwater harvesting.

London, UK, 2004 – (under construction)
Client: Project Grande (Guernsey) Limited

1　View from Hyde Park.
2　Aerial view.

1

2

Ching Fu Group Headquarters

This office design for the HQ for Ching Fu, one of Taiwan's leading shipbuilders, is aimed at uniting the various activities of the group in one area close to the edge of Kaohsiung Bay and within an emerging science and business park.

The design is based on a series of repeated 8.5 m x 8.5 m orthogonal grids with cores located at either end of the structure. The ground-floor and first-floor levels house the lobby as well as an exhibition area and a 100-seat auditorium. The remaining eight storeys contain company offices. The upper three storeys are set back from the façade to make a terrace area for staff. One of the key features of the building is the design of the 'boxes' which form 'floating' extensions of the office space at different levels and to make meeting rooms and private office areas.

Because of the intensely hot summers and monsoon climate in Kaohsiung, the roof is made up of louvres which help to reduce heat gain on the building envelope and give a distinctive finish to the building. Exposed columns and large extractor funnels in vivid primary colours echo the Pompidou Centre design by expressing the system of building elements, as well as acknowledging the Ching Fu Group's own colours.

Kaohsiung, Taiwan, 2005 – 7
Client: Ching Fu Shipbuilding Co. Ltd,
WeeLee International Co. Ltd,
WeeLee International Tourism
Management Co. Ltd
Co-architects: HOYA Architects & Associates

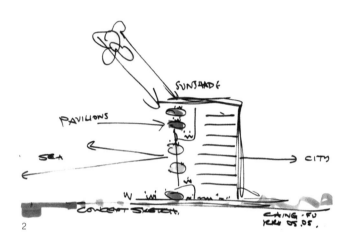

1 Waterfront elevation (page left).
2 Concept sketch.
3 Sketch of elevation.

Metropolitana Linea 1 – Santa Maria del Pianto

This new underground station for Metropolitana Linea 1 is close to the north entrance of the cemetery of Santa Maria del Pianto and between the stations at Poggioreale and Capodichino. The design creates a transport hub which incorporates a bus station, parking for up to 1,500 vehicles and a concourse for arriving and departing passengers incorporating a ticket sales facility, restaurants and retail. The station will cater for upwards of 6,000 passengers per hour, helping to absorb rush-hour traffic as well as visitors to the cemetery itself, particularly on Sundays and festivals. The new hub will provide a catalyst for the regeneration of a neglected, relatively inaccessible area and create a new point of access for the city. A public square provides a meeting point for those passengers using the bus interchange and metro station.

The entrance is visually marked by a sculptural roof overhang. A gradual transition from the interior of the station to the external public realm is created by a design which allows natural light to penetrate the inner zones.

Naples, Italy, 2006 – (ongoing)
Client: Metropolitana di Napoli

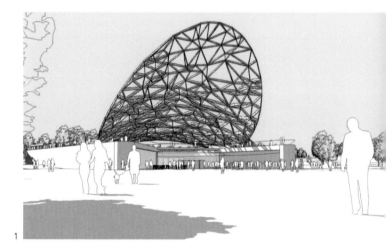

1

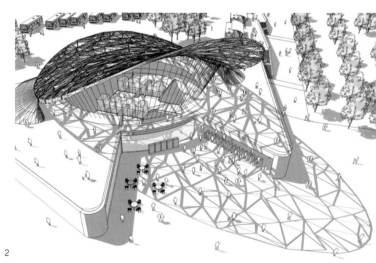

2

1 & 2 Computer model showing views towards station entrance.

Parc1

**Seoul, South Korea,
2004 – (under construction)
Client: Skylan Properties
Co-architect: Samoo Architects & Engineers**

Located in the Yeouido district of Seoul, Parc1 is a 4.6-hectare site containing a mixed-used commercial complex that will integrate office, retail and hotel accommodation with public transport. Together with existing and nearby emerging residential developments, Parc1 will form a new urban hub in Seoul. The masterplan is organised to respond to existing views of the city grain and massing, as well as vehicular access and pedestrian movement.

Facing Yeouido Park the two office towers, one 302m and the other 226m in height, accentuate the existing skyline and take full advantage of the panoramic views of Seoul and the mountains beyond. The towers will create a landmark structure showing the western entrance to the city from the airport. The retail centre will provide 24/7 public facilities for the new complex and its scale will mediate between the differing heights of the office towers and the hotel.

1 View of original scheme.
2 Aerial view of final scheme.

Barangaroo

RSHP originally took part in a major design competition in 2005 for a masterplan for the redevelopment of the foreshore area of East Darling Harbour on the edge of central Sydney. The competition sought proposals that would fit within the context of existing developments and form a new public water edge to the city. The project was guided by the need for a significant waterfront precinct providing a mix of commercial, retail, hotel and residential and leisure uses. The development would form the final major piece of Sydney's CBD, have a carbon-neutral footprint and provide around 50% of green, open space in the area supported by a strong community-orientated infrastructure.

The first phase of the now renamed 'Barangaroo' development, described by the masterplan, was tendered for development rights in 2008. RSHP – as part of a team led by Lend Lease – produced a detailed masterplan arranged as a fan of buildings creating spaces and views opening outwards to the west and helping to reconnect Sydney to its western waterfront. Energy-efficient design and on- and off-site renewable energy generation maintains the project's original carbon-neutral aspiration. The scheme was chosen as the preferred proposal at the end of 2009.

Sydney, Australia, 2005 – (ongoing)
Client: New South Wales Government
/ Lend Lease
Co-architects: Lipmann Associates + PTW

1 Plan (below).
2 Model scale 1:1500.

2

Design for Manufacture Housing

The UK Government's Design for Manufacture competition sought new prototype housing schemes, which would use modern methods of construction (such as prefabrication) to accelerate provision of low-cost, energy efficient, sustainable, high-quality housing.

Using eco-friendly timber panel construction, the design of the Oxley Woods scheme offers generic prefabricated housing with numerous variations to suit different sites and constraints. The prefabricated house takes five days to manufacture, with one truck required to deliver a single house, 24 hours to erect on site and waterproof and is complete within two weeks. The houses are easily adaptable, so that they can change with the varying lifestyles and family demands of their occupants over time.

The serviced spaces of these houses – including bathrooms, kitchens and heating / lighting centres – are standardised across the range of house types. Each home has an a 'EcoHat' chimney that gathers warm air from service zones – such as the kitchen – and channels it back into the living room.

**Milton Keynes, UK,
2005 – (under construction)
Client: English Partnerships with developer
George Wimpey South Midlands**

1 Drawings of different house types.
2 House assembly drawings.
3 General view of Oxley Woods development (below, page right).
4 Typical house under construction over 24-hour period (overleaf).

The superstructure of each house takes five days to manufacture in the factory, 24 hours to assemble on site (once the foundations have been prepared) and two weeks to fit out.

Ivan Harbour 'Houses can be expanded and modified to suit the changing needs of the owners.'

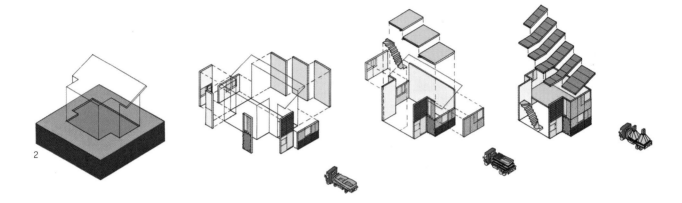

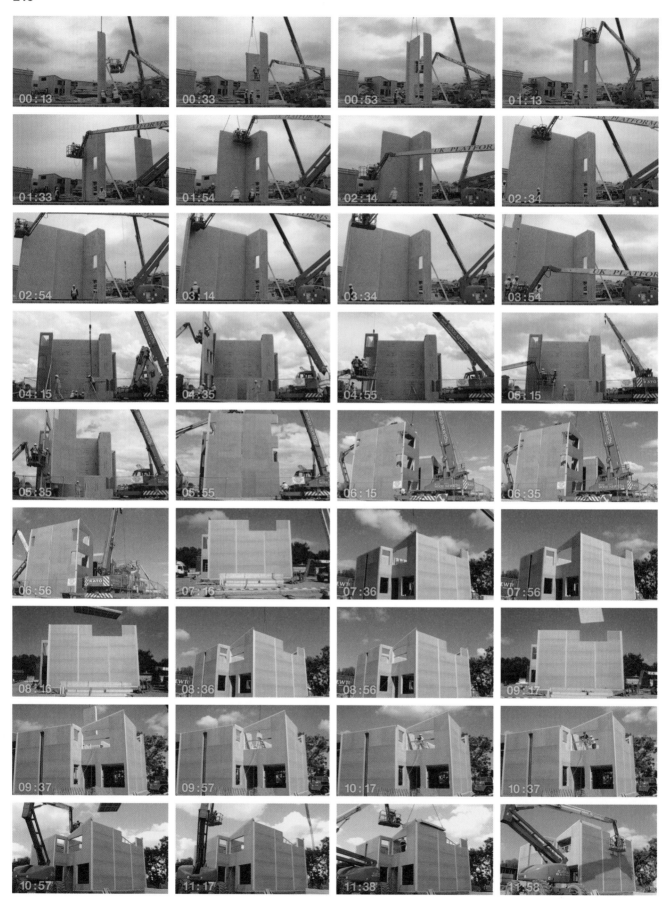

Building a house in 24 hours.

5

6

5 Streetscape showing different house types.
6 View from adjacent park.
7 Light and generous living space.

NEO Bankside

NEO Bankside is set within the Bankside area of the South Bank in London, where a wide range of cultural, business and residential communities have co-existed in an intricate web of streets dating from medieval times. Occupying a complex, irregular space with particular urban constraints, the scheme is located close to the River Thames, directly opposite the west entrance to one of London's most popular cultural buildings, Tate Modern, and its proposed extension.

NEO Bankside will comprise 229 residential units in five separate buildings ranging from six to 24 storeys within landscaped gardens. The units vary from studios to four-bedroom penthouses. Of the total units, 32 are shared equity, with a substantial provision of affordable housing to be provided on separate sites. In addition to residential accomodation covering 28,600 m², retail units are provided at ground level with a total area of 3,353 m².

The configuration of the buildings creates a new marker for the area. The five individual buildings step in height in response to neighbouring properties. Planning permission was granted in 2007 and work to deliver the first phase of the scheme is now well underway.

**London, UK, 2006 – (under construction)
Client: GC Bankside LLP (a Joint Venture between Native Land and Grosvenor)**

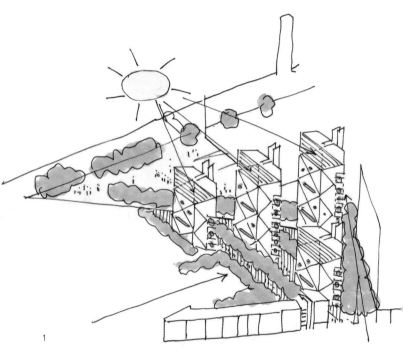

1

1 Concept sketch.
2 Model, scale 1:500.

World Conservation and Exhibitions Centre, British Museum

RSHP won a competition in 2007 to design new facilities aimed at significantly improving and enhancing the British Museum's existing infrastructure by providing additional exhibition space, state-of-the-art conservation and science laboratories, storage areas for its study collection and facilities to support its extensive UK and international loans programme.

The challenge was to produce a design that both expresses the contemporary role and world-class standing of the British Museum and also responds to its wider institutional and architectural legacy. The result is a series of four linked pavilions – each of five storeys above basement level – connecting to the main Museum. A fifth pavilion – containing scientific research facilities – is submerged below ground.

When finished in 2013, the development will help to ensure that the Museum can meet its present and future obligation to the collection and to its visitors for many years to come.

Location: London, UK, 2007 – (ongoing)
Client: British Museum

1   Computer-generated view from Montague Place.
2 & 3   Concept sketches.

1

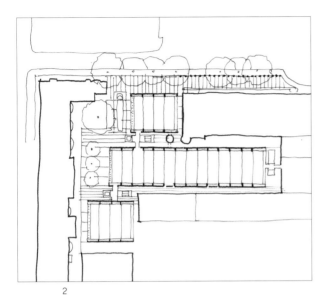

2

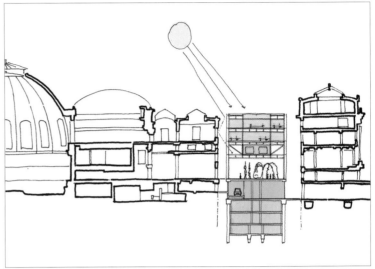

3

Grand Paris

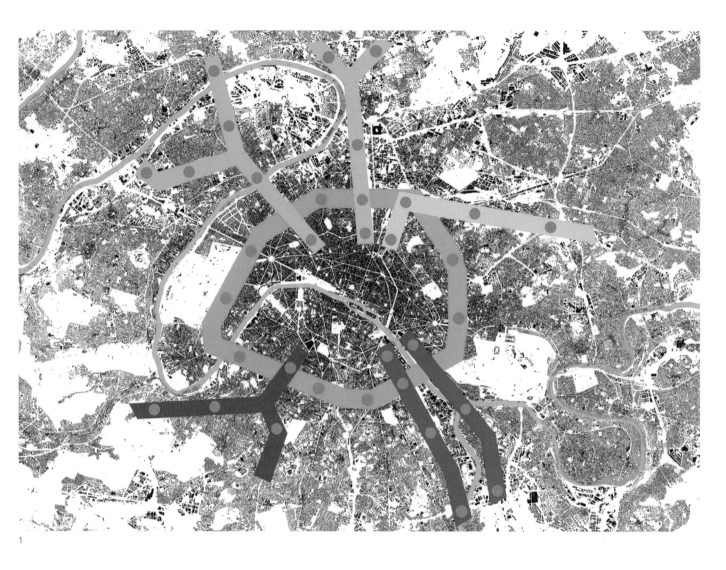

1

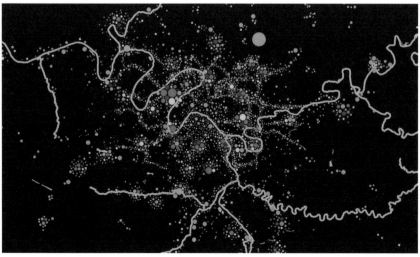

2

1 Proposed metropolitan
armatures for Grand Paris.
2 A strategy for transformation:
1,000 projects –
a multitude of projects
at many different scales.
3 Conceptual model
of Grand Paris.

Paris, France, 2008 – (ongoing)
Client: Ministère de la Culture, France
Team: London School of Economics and Arup

The practice was invited by the French President to study 'Grand Paris' – looking at the future of the French capital as an integrated metropolitan region. A team comprising RSHP, the London School of Economics and Arup was commissioned to address the key social and environmental challenges facing Grand Paris in the 21st century.

As part of an integrated approach to public transport, the team proposed a series of circumferential metro lines linking strengthened poly centres in the Parisian suburbs and reinforcing the existing public transport network. New 'metropolitan armatures' were also proposed, to be constructed over the divisive and inaccessible urban canyons formed by the existing rail lines, housing integrated infrastructure. These would link the centre of the city to the suburbs and also create lateral routes between previously separated neighbourhoods.

RSHP continues to work directly with the French Government to develop a more humane, responsive and ecologically sensitive Paris for the 21st century.

The team proposed 10 key principles for the Paris region:

1 **Restructure the governments of the metropolis.**
2 **Build Paris on Paris ('The Compact City').**
3 **Create a truly metropolitan public transport network.**
4 **Reinforce a polycentric metropolitan Paris.**
5 **Build balanced communities.**
6 **Rebalance the regional economy.**
7 **Bridge the physical barriers of the city.**
8 **Create a metropolitan open space network.**
9 **Reduce the environmental footprint of metropolitan Paris.**
10 **Invest in high quality urban design and architecture.**

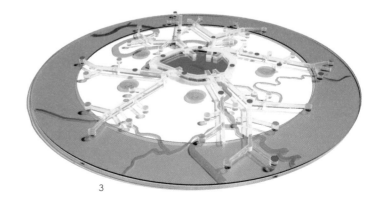

3

Da-An Park

Taipei, Taiwan, 2008 – (ongoing)
Client: Yuan Lih Construction
Co-architects: CT Chen Architects
and Associates

These two towers are located on the edge of Da-An Park in central Taipei. Each tower is approximately 140 m tall, and will – when completed – be among the tallest residential buildings in Taipei. Apartments will range from 400 – 1,000 m². Two smaller apartment units form each storey at the lower levels of the towers while towards the top, each floor is formed of a single, large apartment. All apartments have panoramic views of the park with generous external terraces which articulate the park-side elevations. The north and south elevations are articulated by projecting windows and external shading elements while the east elevations are accentuated by slender, colourful stair cores.

The areas around the base of the towers will provide a new, landscaped public space in the Da-An Park neighbourhood, complemented by two open-air public galleries facing onto adjoining public gardens.

View of the residential towers.

Grand Hotel

This proposed hotel development is on the site of a former theatre building in Beirut at the corner of Rue Emir Bechir and Rue Syre which had fallen into disrepair during recent years. It was acquired for refurbishment as a landmark hotel for the city. RSHP's design approach retains much of the structure of the original building as well as the existing street façade, while adding a striking contemporary building format of stepped, pavilion-like structures supported by pilotis, addressing Riad El Hosn Square and an emerging collection of new buildings to the north west.

The proposal will deliver up to 83 guest rooms of various sizes as well as a ballroom, pool area restaurants, cafés and bars. A key feature will be a huge, naturally-lit pool area occupying the former theatre auditorium with access to a garden area containing three smaller pools.

The development reflects a growing confidence in Beirut as a key business and tourist destination.

Beirut, Lebanon, 2009 – (ongoing)
Client: Solidere

1

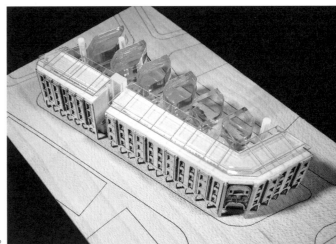

2

1 View of hotel from north west.
2 Model, scale 1:1000.

Tadawul – Saudi Stock Exchange

The design of this 200 m-high, 52-storey headquarters building in the King Abdullah Financial District of Riyadh responds to a masterplan for a new zone in the city and is at the edge of a proposed cluster of tall buildings. It aims to create an individual and unique identity on the city skyline for the new building.

The design addresses the extreme climate of Riyadh by creating a building which has a protective outer layer that shades the working and communal areas inside. The external screening draws upon traditional elements of Arabian architecture but with a contemporary reinterpretation. The arrangement of internal spaces – with wide, relatively column-free and self-supporting 27 m floorplates and communal gardens on every fifth floor – seeks to engender a sense of community and a positive working environment for stock exchange employees as well as those working in the offices above. The top five storeys of the building form a spectacular internal garden area for staff to meet and relax.

Riyadh, Saudi Arabia, 2009 (unbuilt)
Client: Tadawul

1

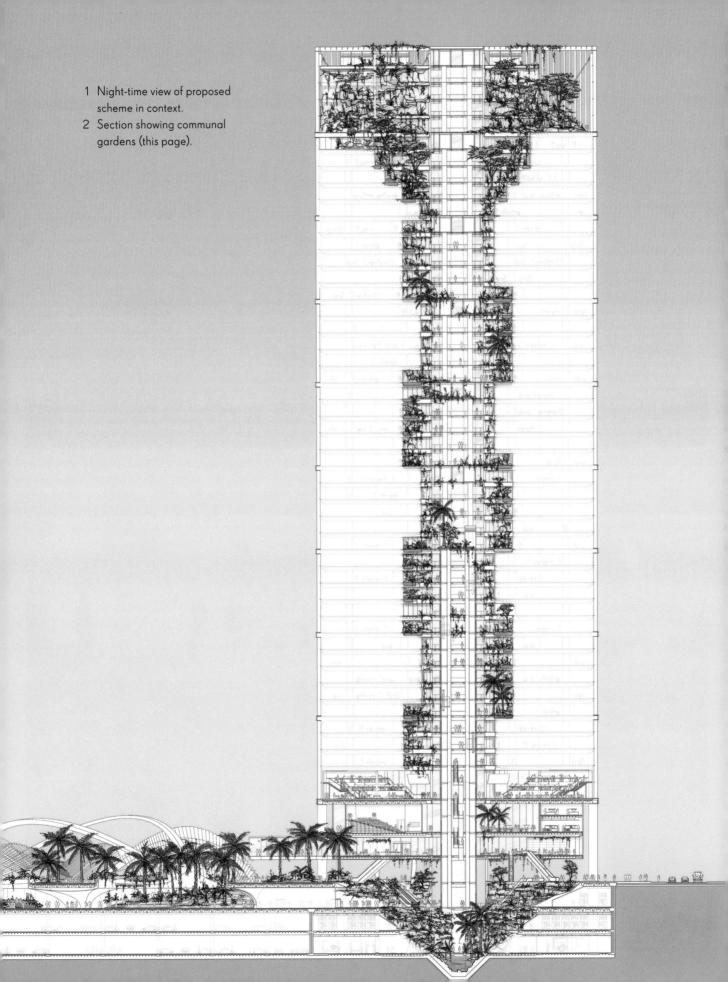

1 Night-time view of proposed
  scheme in context.
2 Section showing communal
  gardens (this page).

GyeongGi Do Provincial Government Offices

1

2

The GyeongGi Do Provincial Government is seeking to relocate its existing headquarters facilities to a new HQ building on a site approximately 20km from the South Korean capital, Seoul.

RSHP was invited to compete for a preliminary design proposal which provides 100,000 m^2 of space for government offices and multi-functional facilities in a complex that is also easily accessible to visiting members of the public. As well as office space and a government assembly building, the design incorporates a multi-purpose conference hall for public – as well as government – use and an expansive public plaza, open 24-hours, which provides a seamless transition between the external and internal spaces of the scheme. The development aims to optimise the use of natural and renewable sources of energy to achieve LEED 'Platinum' level in sustainable design.

The masterplan also offers a significant element of other mixed-used developments, including cultural and recreational facilities, around the headquarters complex. The design approach demonstrates the potential for creating major public schemes which blur the relationship between man-made and natural landscapes and encourage greater public participation in government activities.

Seoul, South Korea, 2009 (unbuilt)
Client: GyeongGi Do Provincial
Government, South Korea
Co-architect: Gansam & Partners

3

4

1 Section.
2 Aerial view.
3 Interior view.
4 Model, scale 1:2000.

Film direction: Marina Willer
Production: Beatrice Vears
Photography: Jonathan Clabburn
and Melissa Duarte
Duration: 8'15"

INSIDE

E OUT

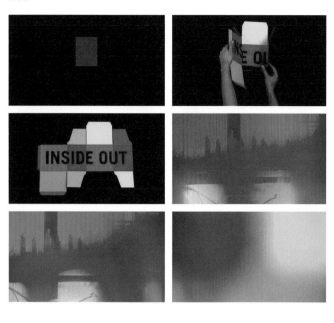

Richard Rogers 'There was a wonderful oath which Greek citizens made when they became citizens – "We leave this city not less but greater, better and more beautiful than it was left to us."'

Tracy Meller 'We all work here because we fundamentally believe in the same kind of things, the same ethos if you like: the desire to make places that enrich people's lives, not just buildings that are monuments to great architecture.'

Ann Miller 'I am just thinking about the difference between a building and what architecture is and I tend to think of it as being something that is uplifting. When you see children playing in a wonderful space, we might know it's a great space because of all the effort, and cost, perhaps, that have gone into it. But children, they are not even aware of it, they seem to sense it.'

Graham Stirk 'Logic will lead you somewhere but will only give you an understanding of operationally how to deal with the logistics of a problem. It doesn't lead you to a kind of poetic response.'

Ivan Harbour 'The process of architecture is not an island, it involves community. It is not a question of sitting in a corner, it is actually a question of having a discussion about everything from the politics of where you are about to do the work, to what it's going to give back to the community that you are putting it in.'

Richard Rogers 'Architecture is measured against the past, you build in the present and you try to imagine the future.'

Graham Stirk 'It is the nature of how buildings dialogue with those people that are not using them, so it isn't good enough to be able to say we have a client who is happy.'

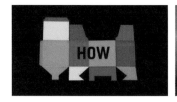   

Ivan Harbour 'The rigour, the science, they are your tools, really, but the way they are put together, that's the thing that has an element of intuition about it, an element of art.'

Jack Newton 'I have never been in an institution where everyone is so positive and, in a funny way, it probably has an influence on the fact that our work has always got this kind of brightness, this lightness of touch.'

Ivan Harbour 'We have a constitution, the broad headlines are very clear; they are about being human and having a civic responsibility.'

Graham Stirk 'The only thing that is constant is change. The fact that something is able to be flexible enough to respond to many, many different conditions.'

Georgina Robledo 'We always say there's nothing new, so we're always rethinking and rebuilding thoughts.'

Richard Rogers 'A church is only sometimes a church. A church may become a nightclub. So, what is a church, what is a nightclub? What's a house, what's an office? You create structures which indicate how change can take place.'

Graham Stirk 'We explore an approach which might begin life as an aspiration, but one still has to give it form, to give it image, to give it geometry, rhythm and scale.'

Richard Rogers 'We live to live and work is part of living.'

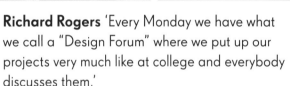

Richard Rogers 'Every Monday we have what we call a "Design Forum" where we put up our projects very much like at college and everybody discusses them.'

Ivan Harbour 'We don't want people who just say Yes, Yes, Yes. We want people who are awkward, particular, and passionate; you know these things are really important.'

Andrew Morris 'Part of developing and motivating the team ethic is to make sure that the management of the practice is just as transparent as our buildings.'

Richard Rogers

Since founding Richard Rogers Partnership in 1977 – which became Rogers Stirk Harbour + Partners in 2007 – Richard Rogers has gained international recognition as an architect and urbanist. He is the 2007 Pritzker Architecture Prize Laureate, recipient of the 1985 RIBA Gold Medal and the 2006 Golden Lion for Lifetime Achievement (La Biennale di Venezia). He was knighted in 1991, made a life peer in 1996 and a Member of the Order of the Companions of Honour (CH) in 2008.

In 1995, he was the first architect to be invited to give the BBC Reith Lectures – a series entitled 'Cities for a Small Planet' – and in 1998 was appointed by the Deputy Prime Minister to chair the UK Government's Urban Task Force. He was Chief Advisor on Architecture and Urbanism to the Mayor of London, Ken Livingstone and a design advisor to the current Mayor of London, Boris Johnson. He has also been an advisor to the Mayor of Barcelona's Urban Strategies Council.

Richard's ability to bring together the best team for a job, coupled with a clear design focus and intuitive understanding of how cities and people interact, has ensured a string of successful commissions and projects and made a major impact on contemporary architecture. Key projects include the Centre Pompidou, Paris, Lloyd's of London and Terminal 4 Barajas Airport, Madrid.

Graham Stirk

Graham Stirk joined the practice in 1983, was made a director in 1988 and a senior director in 1995. He has been involved in the design of a number of prestigious UK and worldwide projects. In 2007 the name of the practice was changed in recognition of his and Ivan Harbour's contributions.

Graham – together with Ivan and Richard Rogers – is evolving the practice's language of design, to create sustainable and thought-provoking architecture. His intellectually rigorous approach to the analysis and interpretation of a client brief and site informs the process and form of architecture to create functional, flexible and elegant designs.

Graham has brought innovative, rational and clear design leadership to many of the practice's high-profile projects including three Stirling Prize shortlisted designs – Lloyd's Register of Shipping, 88 Wood Street and Bodegas Protos. Other projects include: the Leadenhall Building; NEO Bankside; One Hyde Park; and an extension for The British Museum to provide a flexible series of exhibition and conservation spaces.

In addition, Graham has contributed to the design of several key masterplanning projects including Potsdamerplatz, Berlin and Paddington Basin, London.

Ivan Harbour

Ivan Harbour joined the practice in 1985. He cut his teeth on Lloyd's of London and subsequently led the design of the European Court of Human Rights and Bordeaux Law Courts. He was made a director in 1993 and senior director in 1998. In 2007 the name of the practice was changed in recognition of Ivan's and Graham Stirk's contributions. Together with Richard Rogers, they are evolving the practice's language of design, to create sustainable and thought-provoking architecture for the future.

Ivan has considerable experience of directing complex projects both large and small and of many different types. Projects designed and realised under his supervision include: Barangaroo masterplan, Sydney; Maggie's Centre, London (2009 Stirling Prize winner); 300 New Jersey Avenue offices, Washington DC; Parc1, a mixed-use development in Seoul; Oxley Woods, sustainable and affordable housing in Milton Keynes, UK; Terminal 4 Barajas Airport, Madrid (2006 Stirling Prize winner); National Assembly for Wales, Cardiff; law courts in Antwerp; Minami Yamashiro School, Kyoto, Japan; Mossbourne Community Academy, London; Ching Fu Shipping Headquarters and R9 Metro Station, Kaohsiung, Taiwan.

These projects have all been recognised by either national, European or international awards.

Andrew Morris

Since joining the practice in 1982, Andrew Morris has gained experience at many different levels in a wide range of projects. He has been responsible for the co-ordination of multidisciplinary design teams as co-director on: The Millennium Dome, Lloyd's Register of Shipping, 88 Wood Street and One Hyde Park, in London, The Designer Retail Outlet in Kent and the Marine Hotel in Salcombe, Devon and has led teams in major urban regeneration projects in Cambridge, Chelmsford, Southampton, and Wembley.

Andrew has a particular interest in commercial / legal aspects of the practice and is senior commercial director, responsible for negotiating and agreeing RSHP's appointments, overseeing design management and contract administration and playing a major role in managing the practice.

He promotes the practice's vision in relation to new methods of procurement and design management. He has sat on a number of industry bodies dedicated to improving the construction industry including the Design and Build Foundation and was a founding member of the Collaboration for the Built Environment. He is the professional practice co-ordinator for 5th Year Architecture Masters students at the Royal College of Art, London.

Mike Davies

Mike Davies has worked with Richard Rogers and the practice for almost 40 years and has been involved with virtually all the projects it has undertaken. He worked on the Pompidou Centre, Paris in the 1970s and was project architect for the adjacent Institute for Research & Co-ordination in Acoustics & Music (IRCAM). On returning to the UK he worked on Lloyd's of London, INMOS, and the Europier / Terminal 1 expansion at London's Heathrow Airport.

Mike's specific expertise includes masterplanning and urban design, science, technology, research and development. He was project director for the strategic masterplans for the City of Dunkirk and the Royal Docks and the Greenwich Peninsula in London, as well as leading the team for the Lower Manhattan East River project, New York.

Mike led the initial strategic design team on the redevelopment of the Javits Convention Centre, and 175 Greenwich Street, World Trade Center site, in New York. At Canary Wharf, London, he was director of the initial proposals for Riverside South and led the masterplanning of Wood Wharf. Mike was project director for the Millennium Dome, London and for Terminal 5 at Heathrow Airport and is currently project director for 'Grand Paris'.

In 2000, he was awarded a CBE for services to architecture.

Lennart Grut

Lennart Grut is the director in charge of overseeing the management of most the practice's projects outside the UK as well as the RSHP offices in Spain and Japan. His role includes organising and managing multidisciplinary teams in multi-lingual environments to ensure delivery of projects within a wide variety of cost and time constraints, while respecting the exacting quality and environmental standards set by the practice.

He has particular expertise in the planning and design of major airport projects and has been director in charge of Terminal 5, Heathrow Airport, London as well as Terminal 4 Barajas Airport, Madrid. More recently he has been involved in setting up the practice's new work in Mexico, Lebanon and China as well helping maintain a continued presence in Europe, in particular Italy and France.

Lennart oversees the Digital Design, IT and Communications departments at the practice.

Richard Paul

Richard Paul has wide-ranging international experience as a director with Rogers Stirk Harbour + Partners and has managed large teams of architects on major schemes worldwide.

After the competition for Shanghai Pudong International Airport, Richard co-led the team that won the competition for Shanghai Expo 2010 to design a new mixed-use urban district.

Richard has a well-recognised reputation for outstanding leadership and innovation. He promotes excellence in the design of sustainable architecture which fundamentally underpins the RSHP design philosophy. An example of this can be seen at Chiswick Park, London, which is an energy-efficient, low-cost, sustainable environment which set the benchmark for this building typology throughout the UK and Europe. More recently, Richard championed the design of 175 Greenwich Street, a 75-storey, mixed-use office building on the site of the World Trade Center in New York. He is currently directing the design evolution of Canary Riverside.

Richard was previously a board director of Foster + Partners where he worked on the Hong Kong and Shanghai Bank Headquarters in Hong Kong, where he also lived for a number of years.

Mark Darbon

Mark Darbon joined the practice in 1990 and became a director in 2001. Mark has experience of working on a wide range of projects from large-scale urban regeneration developments to medium-scale schemes including the Channel 4 Headquarters in London, the Learning Resource Centre for Thames Valley University in Slough and Potsdamerplatz in Berlin. He was project architect for the Montevetro apartments in Battersea, LIFT White City housing scheme and health centre in London, the Designer Retail Outlet Centre in Kent and Tower Bridge House in London. He is currently leading the design of a major headquarters building for BBVA-Bancomer in Mexico City.

Mark's involvement in significant competition entries such as the Fourth Grace, Liverpool and Silvertown Docks, London has greatly contributed to his expertise in urban regeneration. More recently, he has led masterplanning projects such as Woolston Shipyard in Southampton, Convoy's Wharf in London and a major new proposal for the station area of Cambridge.

Mark was key to the success of these projects with his highly flexible approach to design, an understanding of the complexities of each site, and a high degree of collaboration with external consultants.

Amarjit Kalsi

Amarjit Kalsi is a director at Rogers Stirk Harbour
+ Partners and has worked on a number
of key projects including Lloyd's of London.
He is currently director in charge of two new
subway stations in Naples: Capodichino Airport
and Santa Maria del Pianto, both designed
as major transport hubs. Previously, Amarjit was
director in charge of the design for the Learning
Resource Centre, Thames Valley University,
Slough, and various projects in France including
Port Aupec, Bordeaux Law Courts and the
European Court of Human Rights, Strasbourg.
London projects include: Terminal 5, Heathrow
Airport; 88 Wood Street; the Millennium Dome,
Greenwich; and Montevetro, a residential
scheme in Battersea.

Amarjit has worked on numerous other projects
worldwide including: the Antwerp Law Courts;
Leuven Train Station; Terminal 4 Barajas Airport,
Madrid; Campus Palmas Altas, Seville; Javits
Convention Center, New York; and the Mantua
Stadium in Italy. He has led the practice's
product design work including a series of bus
shelters and street furniture for Adshel and
Cemusa and a lighting system for Reggiani.

He enjoys design from competition and concept
stages through to detailed design development,
fabrication and construction as well as working
on projects that are both micro and macro
in scale.

Ian Birtles

Ian Birtles joined the practice in 1997, and
having been made associate in 2001 he joined
the board of directors in 2004. Ian began
his career by training with Bristow Burrell & Co,
a Guildford and London-based firm of chartered
accountants. He then moved to the City,
where he spent 10 years working for international
chartered surveyors Gooch & Wagstaff.
In 1997 he was recruited as head of finance
at the practice and is responsible for reporting
to the board on all financial matters.

Ian works closely with the directors on the
financial aspects of all RSHP projects. He was
instrumental in developing the practice's BAA
framework agreement for Terminal 5, Heathrow
Airport and was also part of the management
team for the Spanish joint venture that delivered
Terminal 4 Barajas Airport in Madrid. He is
responsible for setting up and structuring the
practice's various overseas entities and is currently
closely involved in a joint venture in Mexico which
is delivering a new headquarters building for
BBVA-Bancomer.

Ian supports and advises RSHP students
on the financial elements of the RIBA
Part III qualification.

Our belief

The practice of architecture is inseparable from the social and economic values of the individuals who practise it and the society which sustains it. We as individuals are responsible for contributing to the welfare of mankind, the society in which we practise, and the team with whom we work.

Our aims

We aim to produce work which is beneficial to society. We exclude work related directly to war or which contributes to the extensive pollution of our environment.

How we work

In order to do work of the highest quality, we carefully control the size of the office and the selection of our projects. We recognise that work is not an end in itself and that a balanced life must include the enjoyment of leisure and the time to think.

Our charitable ownership

Our Practice is owned by a Charitable Trust. No individual owns any share in the value of the Practice. In this way, private trading and inheritance of shares is eliminated and any residual value is returned to society through the Charitable Trust.

How we are organised

We believe in an equitable and transparent sharing of the rewards of our work. The earnings of the directors are fixed in proportion to those of the lowest paid, fully qualified architect. After reserves and tax, any profits are divided between all of the staff and charities according to publicly-declared principles.

We believe that these arrangements nurture an ethos of collective responsibility to each other, satisfaction in the work we produce and a sense of wider social responsibility.

Charity

A percentage of all profits is donated to charitable causes every year. Each director and employee directs their share of the charitable distribution to a charity of their own choice. Over the years, substantial sums of money have been paid to charitable causes.

7T, Aaron Massingham, Aba Amihyia, Abi Smith, Abigail Ford, ACS, Adam Cossey, Adam James, Adam Jonathan Lee, Adams Kara Taylor, Adamson Associates, ADD, Adele Pascal, Adeline Wee, Adelphine Williams, Aderonke Fadayiro, Adolfo Arellano, Adolfo Preus, Adrian King, Adrian Williams, Advanced Structures, Agroindiro, Ahrends Burton & Koralek, Aida Estaban Millat, Alleen Siu, Ainhoa Abreu Diaz , Ainoa Prats Garcia, Airab Consultant, Akihisa Kageyama, Akimichi Inaba, AKRF, Alan Baxter Associates, Alan Davidson, Alan Saunders Associates, Alan Stanton, Alasdair Macdonald, Alastair Parvin, Alba Fernandez, Alberto Morselli , Alec Vassiliades, Aleksandrina Rizova, Alembic Research, Alessandra Molinari, Alessandro Pierandrei, Alessandro Rizzo Architetto, Alex Ferguson, Alex Franz, Alex Haw, Alex Kaiser, Alex Zimmerman, Alexander Meitlis, Alexandra Onet, Alfonso Galan, Alice Odeke, Alicia Cortell, Alison Cronin, Alison Sampson, Allesandre Pierandrei, Almudena Bustos, Alonso Balaguer y Arquitectos Asociados, Alphons Oberhofer, Amanda Botts, Amanda Deaves, Amanda Levete, Amarjit Kalsi, Amarjit Tamber, AMEC, Amy Haddow, Ana Belen Franco Santa Cruz, Ana Carbonero, Ana Serrano, Anabela Chan, Andrea Parigi, Andrea Whitfield, Andrea Wu, Andrei Saltykov, Andrés Arellano, Andrés Fernández , Andrés Martínez, Andrew Clarkson, Andrew Gallagher, Andrew GrantAssociates, Andrew Holmes, Andrew Jones, Andrew Morris, Andrew Morrison, Andrew Partridge, Andrew Strickland, Andrew Tyley, Andrew Weston, Andrew Wright, Andrew Yek, Andy Bryce, Andy Clayton, Andy Young, Anenmos, Angela Gates, Angela Jackson, Angela Rausch, Angela Van Herk, Ann Miller, Anna Acebillo, Anna Brewer, Anna Herve, Annabel Rootes, Anne Enright, Annette Main, Annie Blackadder, Annie Castle, Annie Wingfield, Anser, Anstey Horne & Co., Anthony C. Baker, Anthony Hunt Associates, Anthony White, Antonia Garcia, Antonio Lamela, Apex/FPD Savills, Appleton, Mechor & Associates, APS Project Management, Architect 5, Ariel Ariel, Arif Azmee Nik, Arif Mehmood, Artesia, Arup, Asanuma Corporation, ASI, Astec Projects, Astrid Osborn, ATAKA Fire Safety Design Office, Atelier 9/ETA, Atelier Claude Bucher, Atelier Hafu Architects, Atelier One, Atkins, Atsu Wada, Atsushi Sasa, Augustine Igbanugo, Avery Agnelli, Avery Howe, Avtar Lotay, AWP, Axtell Yates Hallett, AYH Partnership, B Consultants, B&B Italia, B&FL, BAA, Balfour Beatty, Ballymore, Barbara Faigle, Barbara Perez, Battle McCarthy, BDG/McColl, BDP, BDSP, Beaney Pearce, Beatriz Gomes-Martin, Beatriz Lopez-Diaz, Beatriz Olivares, Bell Fischer, Ben Britz, Ben Nicholls, Ben Ridley, Ben Rogers, Ben Taylor, Benjamin Darras, Benjamin Garcia Saxe, Benjamin Sztainbok, Benjamin Warner, Bernard Ede, Bernard Plattner, Bernie Plaisted, Beth Margolis, Bickerdike Allen Partners, Bidwells, Bill Scanlon, Binnie Black & Veatch, Birgit Scheppenseifen, Birgit Schlösser, BIW, Bjork Haraldsdottir, Bliss Shamhu, BMT Fluid Dynamics, Bo Rogers, Bob Atwal, Bobby Desai, Bodycote Warringtonfire, Boma, BOMA, Bovis Lend Lease, Branch Associates, BRE, Brendan O'Brien, Brendan Roche, Brian Bell, Bright Curtain Metal, British Olympic Association, Bromley by Bow Centre, Broome, Oringdulph, O'Toole, Rudolf & Associates, Brufau y Asociados, Brynley Dyer, Buddy Haward, Bureau d'Etudes, Bureau Van Kerckhove, Buro Happold, Butler & Young, Caireen O'Hagan, Calle 41, Cambridge Architectural Research, Camille Brandon, Campbell Reith Hill, Canary Wharf Contractors, Capita Symonds, Capital & Provident Regeneration, Cardete & Huet Architectes, Carillion, Carl Smith, Carlos Lainer, Carlos Lamela, Carlos Parraga-Botero, Carlos Temprano, Carmel Lewin, Carmen Marquez Barragan, Carmen Pena, Carol Eagles, Caroline Aisida, Caroline Field, Caroline Schmitz, Caroline Washbourne, Carolyn Gembles, Carrick Howell & Lawrence Architects, Carter Ecological, Caryn Rogers, Catherine Martin, Catherine Pease, Catherine Schramm, Catherine Yousefi, Cathie Curran, CB Richard Ellis, Cento Engineering, Central Parking, César López, Cesar Ruiz-Betancourt, CgMs, Chan Meng, Chapman Taylor, Charles Bernard Gagnon, Charles Funke Associates, Charles Meloy, Charles Morris, Chi Park, Chris Curtis,Chris Dawson, Chris Donnington, Chris McAnneny, Chris Udall, Chris Wilkinson, Chrissi Mehmet, Christian Clemares, Christian Dorin, Christian Fenwick Clennell, Christina Houghton, Christine Otther, Christoph Palmen, Christoph Wand, Christopher Chi Lon Wan , Christopher Fincken, Christopher Raven , Chul-Hee Yoon , Chun Jiang, Cindy Liu, CITTA/RTKL, Claas Schulitz, Claire Hughes, Claire Metivier, Claire Verstraete, Clare Holman, Clare Strasser, Clare Thorneycroft, Clark Construction, Claudette Spielmann, Claudia Fischötter, Claudia Hoge, Claudia Rieradevalle, Claudio Cantella, Cleo Swift, Clifford Green, Clodagh Latimer, CMF, Colette Valensi, Colin MacKenzie, Commins Ingemansson, Community Action Network, Concha Estaban , Construcciones Castro, Construction Specifications, Coral Sullivan, Courtney Goldsmith, Co-Young Engineering, Craig Williams, Cressey Wilder Associates, Cristina Munoz, Cristina Sánchez, Croudace Construction, Cundell Johnston & Partners, Cuno Brullman, CW Consultants, Cynthia Leung, Cynthia Poole, Cyril Goodwin, Dagesh Traffic Consultants, Dainihon & Ichikawa Construction, Dalgleish, Dal-Sterling Group, Dan Amin, Dan Howarth, Dan Kiley, Dan Macarie, Dan Pearson Studio, Dan Sibert, Dan Surveyors Office, Daniel Behr, Daniel Boyd, Daniel Crane, Daniel Howarth, Daniel Lewis, Daniel McKenna, Daniel Minder, Daniel Wright, Danielle Demetriou, Dave Giera, David Ardill, David Bartlett, David Bonnett Associates, David Bottos, David Chipperfield, David Collins, David Cotterrell, David Donaldson, David Giera, David Howe, David Jarvis Associates, David John Evans, David Langdon Schumann Smith, David Liu, David Marks, David Marsland, David Merllie, David Morales, David Morrison, David Thom, David Thompson, David WG Bedwell & Partners, Davide Costa, Davis Langdon, Davood Liaghat, Dawn Khajadour, Dawn Moorcroft, Dean Pike, Debbie Nunn, Debis Risk Consult, Delva Patman Associates, Dennis Austin, Dennis Ho, Department Purple, Derek Clapton & Partners, Derek Lovejoy Partnership, Derek Vice, Desirée Dupuy, Desvigne & Dalnoky, Dewi Jones, D-Fine, DFM Competition, Di Hope, Diego Can Lasso, Dinn Associates, Dio Davies, Dirk Krolikowski, DIV A Arkitekter, Divers Jonas, Dmitri Antonyuk, Domenico Lonurno, Domenique Les Begueris, Dominic O'Flynn, Dominic Penrice, Don Gray, Donaldsons, Doris Saatchi, dosAdos, Douglas Keys, Douglas Paul, DP9, Dragados, Drees & Sommer, Drivers Jonas, DSSR, DTZ, Ducibella Venter & Santore, Dumais Japan, Duncan Harbour, Duncan Turner, Duncan Webster, Dundas & Wilson, E.C. Harris, EAG Environ, ECE Projektmanagement, Economic Research Associates, Ed Burgess, Ed Butler, Ed Hiscock, EDCO Design, Edward Erdman, Edward Hutchinson, Eike Becker, Eitetsu Tei, Elaine Nealis, Elantha Evans, Elefant Gratings, Elena Arzua Tourino, Elena Polycarpou, Élida Margitic, Elisa Casciano, Elizabeth Banks Associates, Elizabeth Parr, Elizabeth Post, Elliot Boyd, Ema Ferraz, Eme Essien, Emilia Alonso, Emily White, Emma England, Emma McQueenie, Emma Tynan, Enrico Bougleux, Enrique Azpilicueta , Enrique Hermosa-Lera, Environ, Equation Lighting Design, Equipe Espace, Eric Holt, Eric Jaffrès, Erica Reeve, Erick Maas Waring , Erika Skabar, Ernest Griffiths, Ernest Lowinger, Ernesto Bartolini, ES Associates, ESD, Esther Bradbury, Esther Crespo Alba, Estudio Lamela, Eva Clark, Eva Jiricna , Eva Utrera, Eversheds, Expanded, Expedition Engineering, Faber Maunsell, Fabian Draeger, Fabiana Chirivi, Fabienne Eymard, Façade Hoists, Fai Tsang, Faidra Matziaraki, Faithful & Gould, Far Eastern Construction Company, Far Eastern General Contractor, Farhat Parveen, Fas Ali, FCC, Fedra, Fehr & Peers, Felicity Thomas, Felix Hammond, Felix J Samuely & Partners, Ferrovial Agroman, FG Minter, Fhecor Ingenieros Consultores, Fiona Charlesworth, Fiona Galbraith, Fiona Gallagher, Fiona Hurst, Fisher Marantz Stone, Flack & Kurtz, Flavio Marano, Fleur Treglown, Florian Eames, Florian Fischötter , Fola Fakunmoju, Foster + Partners, FPD Savills Knight Frank, Francesco Draisci, Francis Golding, Francisco López de Blas, Francisco Martin, Francisco Rojo, Francisco Sanjuán, Franck Hammoutene Architecte, Francois Barat, Francoise Gouinguenet, Frank Breheny, Frank Maione, Frank Peacock, Freda Man Chong Yuen, Friedrich Wagner, Fuji Sound, Fujita Construction, Fuller Peiser, Future Systems, FX Fowle Architects/A Epstein & Sons International, G3 Tecnics, G33, GA Hanscomb Partnership, Gabby Reilly , Gabinete, Galliford Northern, García de los Reyes, Gardiner & Theobald, Gareth Lewis, GEC, Genelle Mackie, Gennaro Picardi, Gensler, Geoff Denslow, Geoffrey Taylor, George Wimpey South Midlands, George Xydis, Georgie Wolton, Georgina Ioannou, Georgina Robledo Padilla, Georgina Savva, Gerald Eve/RPS, German de la Torre, Gethin Hooper, GIA, Gianfranco Franchini, Gianmaria Givanni, Gillespies, GL Francois, Gleeds, Glenn Busch, GMJ, GN Haden and Sons, Gordon Cullen, Gordon Ingram Associates, Graham Anthony, Graham Fairley, Graham McDougall, Graham Simpson, Graham Stirk, Grands Travaux de Marseilles, Grant & Partners, Grant Associates, Gregoris Patsalosavvis, Gregory McLean, Grey Associates, Grieves Associates, Grimley J R Eve, Grupo JG, Gurjit Suri, Gustavo Rios, Guy Scott, GVA Grimley , Gwen Evans, GWP Associates, H Bressloff Associates, Hal Currey, Halcrow Fox & Associates, Halcrow Yolles, Hamilton Associates, Hancock Design Co-ordinates, Han-Il, Hann Tucker, Hannah Carline , Hanna Olin Limited, Hans-Peter Bysaeth, Hariet Watson , Harriet Forrest, Harvinder Gabhari, Hay Barry & Partners, Hayden's Tree & Woodland Management Services, Hayes Davidson, Hazama Joint Venture, Hazel Sutherland, HC Yu, HCA, Heeri Song, Heiko Renninger, Helen Brunskill, Helen Pravda, Helene Diebold, Helga Schlegel, Hendrik Monbaliu, Henrietta Salvesen,Henry Fletcher, Henry Okello, Herkrishan Sohal, HH Angus & Associates, Hideyuki Yamashita, Hilde Depudyt, Hilson Moran Partnership, Hiroshi Hibio, Hiroshi Kawana, Hiroshi Naruse, Hiroyuki Takahashi, Hiroyuki Yoshikawa, HKS Architects, Hoare Lea, Hochiki, HOK, Honey Brothers, Hosser Hass & Partner, Housing & Economic Development Agency, Howard Stein Hudson, HOYA Architects & Associates, HR Wallingford, Hugh Chapman, Hughes Associates, Hulley & Kirkwood Consulting Engineers, Hundt & Partner, Hunt Dobson Stringer, Hurley Robertson & Associates, Husna Daya, Hutter Jennings & Titchmarsh, Huw Turner, Hyder Hydrological & Sewerage, Hyland Edgar Driver, Ian Birtles, Ian Davidson, Ian Foot, Ian Gibson, Ian Hopton, Ian Martin, Ian White Associates, Ian Wright, Idom, Ignacio González, Ignacio Zamorano, Ilaria Benuci, ILKUN C&C Architects, Illona Jobski, Iñaki Díez Aguirre, Inés Salvatierra, Ingérop, Ingleby Trice Kennard, Ingrid Brooke-Barnett, Ingrid Morris, INITEC, Initec, Inma Pedregosa, Institut für Fassadentechnik, Interbuild, Interfaces, Inuzuka Engineering, Irie Miyake Architects, Irini Kiladiti, Isabel Lorenzo, Isabel Vergara, IT Ingegneria dei Trasporti, Iván Cordero, Iván García, Ivan Harbour, Iván Pajares, Iwao Takeuchi, J Roger Preston & Partners, J&JJ Stanford, J2C Ingénierie - Bureau d'Etudes Techniques, Jack Newton, Jackie Hands, Jackie Moore, Jacopo Venerosi Pesciolini, Jacqueline Samuels, Jacqueline Yeung, Jacques Fendard, Jaime Cantero, Jaime Sicilia, Jakem AG, Jakob Gate, Jakob Hense, James Chapman, James Curtis, James Finestone, James Gott, James Leathem, James Longley & Co, James McGrath,, James Philips, James Stopps, James Weir, Jamie Troughton, Jan Dunsford, Jan Güell Rottlan, Jan Kaplicky, Jan Sircus, Jane Donnelly, Jane Duckworth, Jane Hannan, Jane Kille, Jane Taylor, Janet Jack, Janette Mackie, Jaros Baum & Bolles, Jasmin Unwin, Jason Garcia Noonan, Jaspa Kalsi, Javier Ampuero , Javier Calvo, Javier Esteban, Javier Hernández, Javier López, Javier Muñiz, Jayne Fisher, JBB, Jean Huc, Jeffrey Goodlad, Jennifer Lang, Jenny Jones, Jenny Lowe, Jenny Stephens, Jens Weiler, Jeon & Associates, Jerome Edwards, Jesse Hindle, Jessica Morrow, Jessica Reynolds, Jesús Hernández, Jesús Municio, JG y Asociados, Jiang Chun, Jill Anderson, Jim Allan Design, Jim Huffman, Jimmy Abatti, Jimmy Hung, Jinbok Wee, JMP, Jo Murtagh, Jo Walters, Joanna Beck, Joanna Pencakowski, Jo-Anne Alldritt, Jo-Anne Cowen, Joanne Walters, Joannes Cristian Du Plessis, Joaquín Vaquero, Jochen Tombers, Jodie Banfield, Joe Crosier, Johanna Lohse, John Allen Consulting/Mott MacDonald, John Andrews, John Bradley Associates, John Cannon, John Colvin, John Dawson, John Denehy, John Doggart, John Evans, John Hawkes, John Höpfner, John Lacey, John Lowe, John Lyall, John McAslan, John McElgunn, John McFarland, John O'Loughlin, John Sisk & Sons, John Smith, John Sorcinelli, John Vine, John Webb, John Young, Jolyon Drury, Jon Mercer, Jon Steed, Jonathan Voss, Jonathan Webb, Jones Lang LaSalle, Jorge Gomendio, Jorge González , Jorge Jover, Jorge Keipo, Jorge Palomero, José Aguilar, José Carlos Díez, José Julián Horcajo, Jose Llerena, Josef Gartner, Josefina Vago, Joseph Jamieson, Joseph Park , Josh Wilson, Joveria Baig, Joy Smith , Joynes Pike & Associates, JTS, Juan Laguna Roquero, Juan Molina Morales, Juanjo Carrancedo, Judith Bowdler, Judith Raymond, Judy Bing, Judy Taylor, Julia Barfield, Julia Moran, Julian Chen, Julian Coward, Julianna Coleman, Julie Parker, Julio Moreno, Jun Ito, Justin Lau, Justine Harvey, Kai Design Office, Kaiser Bautechnik, Kajima, KAJIMA Corporation, Kandor, Radii, Karen Frimin-Cooper, Karen Murray, Karenna Wilford, Karin Egge, Karina Voggel, Karoline Kafka, Karoline Marcus, Karsten Schulz, Katarina Jagrova, Katarzyna Ciechanowska, Kate Jardine-Brown, Kate Owens, Katerina Walterspiel, Katherine Ridley, Kathryn Humphreys, Kathy Kerr, Katie Lee, Katie Sipthorp, Katie Sohal, Katrin Dzenus, Kayaba Industry, Kazu Kofuku, KBC, Keith Allison, Kelbaugh & Lee Architects, Kelly Darlington, Kelvin Lowe, Ken Allinson, Ken Rupard, Ken

Smith Landscape Architects, Kenchington Little & Partners, Kenneth Brown, Kenny Tsui, Kenta J Bacas, Kevin Gray, Kevin Larkin, Kevin Lewenden,Khalid Lagnatha, KHK Group, Kia Larsdotter, Kieran Breen, Kim Quazi, Kinna Stallard, Kinnear Landscape Architects, Kirsti Stock, Kirstina Petersen, Kisho Kurokawa Architects, Kitazawasangyo Corporation, Kiyo Sawoaka, Knebel & Schumacher, Knight Frank, Koizumi Sangyo Corporation, Komatsu Wall Industry, Kotobuki, Krishan Pattni, Kristina Manis, Kristina Petersen, Kristy Woodruffe, Krisztina Pasti, Kroll Schiff, Kruger & Mohler, Krystyna Weber, Kunihiko Kariya, Kunimi Hayashi, Kyle Stewart, Kyoko Tomioka, Kyung Baik, Laing Management Joint Venture, Laing O'Rourke, Laing South East, Lambert, Smith & Hampton, Land Securities, Landscape Design Partnership, Lang Management Contracting, Langan Engineering & Environmental Services, Langan International, Laura Salisbury, Laura Sandiford, Laura Vega Arroyo, Laura Villa Munoz, Laureano Sanz, Laurie Abbott, Lawrence Halprin, Lawrence Jarvis, Lawrence Leung, Leaside Regeneration, Lee Oliver, Leigh Davenport, Lennart Grut, Leo Fernández, Leonard Williams, Leonardo Pelleriti, Leonardo Valerio, Leonie Pilgrim,Leonie Walker, Leonora Oppenheim , Ler Bing Huan, Lerch Bates & Associates, Leslie Clark Construction, Leslie E. Robertson, Lesos Engineering, Lester Korzelius, Levett & Bailey, Lewis Kinnear, Lifschutz Davidson, Lighting Design Partnership, Lighting Planners Associates, Linda Thompson, Lindsay Gwillam, Lindy Arkin, Linklater & Alliance, Lisa Hudson, Liz Oliver, Liza Duir, Lizzie Többen , LOBB Partnership, London International Sport, Lorenz Frenzen, Lorna Edwards, Lorna Walker Construction, Louise Barnett, Louise Moores, Louise Palomba, Lovejoy, LRS Environmental Engineers, Lucy Dean, Lucy Evans, Lucy Gould, Lucy Hooper, Luis Renau, Luis Vidal, Luke Lowings, Luke Stanley, Lulie Fisher, Lunson Mitchenall, Luz Mery Vargas, LWC, M. Angels Fernández, M3 Consulting, Mace, Maire Engineering, Maite Payà, Malcolm Last, Malcolm McGowan, Mandra Evans, Manens Intertecnica, Maralyn Lai, Marcia Robinson, Marco Carlini, Marco Goldschmied, Marcus Lee, Maria Hadjinicolaou, Maria Loring, Maria Medina Muro, Marienne Hesketh, Marita Schnepper, Mark Chan, Mark Collins, Mark Darbon, Mark Gorton, Mark Guard, Mark Hallett, Mark Newton, Mark Roche, Mark Saunders, Mark Smith, Mark Sutcliffe, Mark Thompson, Marta Cumellas, Marta García-Haro, Martha Gale, Martin Associates, Martin Cook, Martin Kehoe, Martin Richardson, Martin Wells, Martin White, Mary Amos, Mary Le Jeune, Mary Saradinou, Mary Tungay, Masaaki Sekiya, Masaki Kakizoe, Massimo Majowiecki, Massimo Minale, Mat Venn, Mateo Falcone, Mateo Miyar Olaiz, Mathias Kerremans, Mathias Köster, Mathis Osterhage, Matsushita Electric Works, Matt Cooper, Matt Parker, Matt Rees, Matthew David, Matthew Gale, Matthew Hall, Matthew Hesketh, Matthew Lake, Matthew Willmar, Maunsell & Partners, Maureen Diffley, Maurice Brennan, Max Fawcett, Max Fordham, Max Townsend, Max Watson, Maxine Campbell, Mayte Martin, MB&A, McAlpine, McBains Building Surveyors, MCLA, McNicholas Construction, Megan Williams, Melanie Elhers, Melon Studios, Melvyn Newell, Mera Taleb, Mercedes Barbero, Mercedes Bolín, MHS Planners, Michael Barth, Michael Branch, Michael Burckhardt, Michael Dowd, Michael Elkan, Michael Gallie & Partners, Michael Grumbridge, Michael Holden, Michael Hughes, Michael Loose, Michael McGarry, Michael McNamara, Michael Nelson, Michael Uchwat, Michaelangelo Bonvino, Michail Floros, Michele McSharry, Michelle Kaye, Michelle O'Neill, Michiko Sumi, Miguel Ángel Cordero , Mike Davies, Mike Fairbrass, Mike Graham, Mike King, Mike Staples, MillenniumModels, Mills & Reeve, Milton Keynes Highways, Milton Keynes Partnership, Mimi Hawley, Miquel Bargallo, Misako Unno, Misha Smith, Mitsubishi Electric, Mitsubishi Estate Company, Miyuki Kurihara, MKC Consulting, Mm Warburg Schlüter & Co, Monica Da Polenza, Monk Dunstone, Monk Dunstone Associates, Montague Evans, Moon Puig, Moon YH Electrical, Morgan Grenfell Laurie, Morna Robertson, Mott Green & Wall, Mott McDonald, Moya y Asociados, MÜ-HELY, Müller Altvatter + C Barasel, Müller International, Museum of London Archaeology Services, Nadia Kloster, Nadine Rulliere, Naomi McIntosh, Naru Kuroshima, Natalie Clark, Natalie Mayes, Natalie Moore, Natasha Campbell, Natasha Le Comber, Nathan Barr, Nathaniel Lichfield & Partners, Natxo Alonso Paillisse, NBBJ, NECSO, Neil Southard, Neil Swift, Neil Winder, Neil Wormsley, Nerida Hodge, Neville Smith, NHBC, NHK Art, NHK Integrated Technology, Nic Malby, Nichiei Architects, Nicholas Mitchell, Nicholas Pearson Associates, Nick Blake, Nick Burwell, Nick Hancock, Nick White, Nick Zervoglos, Nicky Van Oosten, Nicole Bourke, Nigel Craddock, Nigel Greenhill, Nina Freedman, Nini Cheng, Nippon Steel Corporation, Nisha Sing, Nomisma, Noriaki Okabe, Noriyuki Takada, Norman Dawbarn, Norman Foster, Northcroft Neighbour & Nicholson, Northgrove Land, NTT Facilities, Nuaire, Nuria Widman, Nurse Engineering, Obayashi Corporation, Obiol, Moya y Asociados, OHL, Olga Curell, Olga Ramírez, Olin Partnership, Oliver Collignon, Oliver Kühn, Olivia Weston, Omniplan Architects, Omnium Technique Européene, Oppenheim Lewis, Osamu Kasagi, Osprey Mott MacDonald, OTEP, OtH, OTRA, Otto Ng, Overseas Bechtel, P4/Lighting Design-Uchihara, PA Technology, Pablo Gabriel Codesido, Pablo Gil, Pablo Querol, Paco Chocano, P. Rutter Crawford, Paloma Uriel Fernandez, Paola Posada, Paolo Vincenzi, Paradigm Housing, Parker Rodriguez, Parkin Heritage & Tourism, Pascal + Watson, Pascale Gibon, Pascale Rousseau, Patricia Sendin, Patricia Vazquez, Patricia Yanes, Patrick Davies, Patrick Klugesherz, Paul Cook, Paul Forbes, Paul Grover, Paul Harrison, Paul Hastings, Paul Johnson, Paul Leverizia, Paul Nelson, Paul Smith, Paul Stelmaszczyk, Paul Thompson, Paul West, Paz Moya, PDD Surveyors, PDF Savills, Pedro Morales, Pedro Ruiz, Pell Frischmann, Penny Collins, Pentagram Design, Peter Angrave, Peter Barber, Peter Davenport, Peter Flack, Peter Gibbons, Peter Jennett, Peter Mahoney, Peter McMunn, Peter Rice, Peter Ryan, Peter St John, Peter Thomas, Peter Ullathorne, Peter Wake, Peter Walker, Peutz & Associates, Phaedra Corrigan, Philip Bernard, Philip Chalmers, Philip Dennis, Philip Gumuchdjian, Philippa Browning, Philippe Dupont, Philippe Robert, Phillippa Wilson, Pierre Botschi, Pik-Yan Luk, PKV Architects, Plowman Craven, PLS Engineering, Pope Brothers, POSCO, Poul Anderson, PPS Group, Pr.Nötzold, Proctor Mathews Architects, Proinosa, Public Outreach, QuBE, R Umezawa, RA Heintges & Associates, Rachel Hart, Rachel Lowe, Rachel McGovern, Rae Whittow-Williams, Rainer Verbizh, Rainer Zimmerman, Raison D'Etre, Ralph T King Associates, Ram Ahronov, Ramboll WhitbyBird, Randle Siddeley, Raquel Borras, Raquel Ortega, Raphaela Potter, Rattee and Kett Limited, Raúl García, Ray MacDonnell, READ Group, Rebecca Ivatts, Receca Marton, REEF Associates, Reef Associates, Rendel + Branch, Renee Searle, Renzo Piano, Resources Engineering Services, Rexon Day, RFR OtH Rhone-Alpes, RG Carter, RG Wilbrey Consultants, Ricardo Fuentes , Riccardo Amati, Rice Francis Ritchie, Richard Ellis, Richard Hodkinson Consultancy, Richard Marley, Richard Marzec, Richard May, Richard Paul, Richard Rogers, Richard Rose-Casemore, Richard Roth Architects, Richard Russell, Richard Soundy, Richard Stanton, Richard Thomas, Rise, RLF, Robert C J Bates & Associates, Robert Ducibella and Philip Santore, Robert Gluckman, Robert Hawker Associates, Robert Luck, Robert Myers, Robert Peebles, Robert Silman Associates, Robert Tavernor, Robert Torday, Robert Webb, Robert White, Roger Huntley, Rogers Patscentre, Rolf Jensen & Associates, Romed Perfler, Ronald Lammerts van Beuren , Ronnie MacLellan, Roo Lam Lau, Rosa García, Rose Gray, Rose Latter, Rosie Eatwell-White, Rosser and Russell, Rowena Fuller, Roxanne Stacey, RP+K Sozietät, RPS Group, RSP Architects, Planners & Engineers, RTKL, Rummel Klepper and Kahl, Rummy Design Associates, Russell Gilchrist, Ruth Elias, Ruth Harrison, RW Models, RWDI, RYBKA, S Y Fung, Sabien Rietjens Oosterwal, Sabine Coldrey, SACYR, Saeki, Sakina Harji, Sally Appleby, Sally Draper, Sally Eaton, Sam Postel, Sam Schwartz Engineering, Samantha Cheong, Samantha Hayden, Samantha Masters, Samantha Wilmore, Samoo Architects & Engineers, Samsung Engineering & Construction, Sandy Brown Associates, Sanekazu Kofuku, Sang Lee, Santa-Rita Arquitectos, Sara Broad, Sara Fernández , Sara Meek, Sarah Bosen, Sarah Custance, Sarah Fitzpatrick, Sarah Granville, Sarah Tweedie, Sarah Wong, Satoshi Aiza, Savant International, Savills, SCENE, Schal Bovis, Schindler, Schmidlin UK, Schmidt-Reuter und Partner, Schumann Smith, Scott Gill , SDG, Seaman Smith, Seamus Conway, SeanDaly , Sean Han, Sean McCarthy, Sebastián Collado, SEGA, Sera Grubb, Serena Croxson, SERETE (Bureau d'Etudes), Sergio Hernández, Sergio Ignacio Cascant, Seth Peterson, Seth Stein, SETIMEG, Setsubi-Sekkei 21/Six Squares, Seung Hoon Han, Shahab Kasmai-Tehran, Sharan Rehill, Sharni Howe, Sharnie Joel, Sharon Henry, Sharples Holden Pasquarelli Architects, Shean Sai, Shean Yu, Shelley Harris, Shen Chiu, Shen Milsom & Wilke, Shimizu Corporation, Shimizu Sports, Shira McLeod, Shiu Lun Lam, Shou Design Office, Shu Zhen Lee, Shunji Ishida, Siemens Dematic, Silke Ackermann, Silvia Fukuoka, Simon Catton, Simon Colebrook, Simon Connolly, Simon Davis, Simon Hamnel, Simon Hart, Simon Miller, Simon Smithson, Simon Tonks, Simon Williams-Gunn, Simone Nugent, Simone Stylli-Roussou, Sinotech Engineering Consultants, Sir Robert McAlpine & Sons, Sir William Halcrow & Partners, Siri Stromme Johansen, SJ Berwin, SK&A Associates, SMWM, Sociedad Centros Comerciales España, Société d'Architecture Bernard Henry, SOGO Consultants, Sole Segura, Sònia Castellò, Sonia Perez Rubio, SONY Facility Service, Sophie Braimbridge, Sophie Covey-Crump, Sophie Filhol, Sophie Nguyen, Sound Research Laboratories, Speirs&Major, Sridevi Gopalaswamy, STBRI, Steer Davies Gleave, Stefanie Hamm, Stephan Obermaier, Stephanie Fox, Stephen Barrett, Stephen Harty, Stephen Le Roith, Stephen Leung, Stephen Light, Stephen MacBean, Stephen McKaeg, Stephen Moorhouse, Stephen Pimbly, Stephen Prestage, Stephen Spence, Stephen Stimson, Stephen Tsang, Steve Martin, Steve Mason, Steve Moxon, Steve Rodrigues, Stig Larsen, Stipe, Stone Developments, Stratford Development Partnership, Structured Environment, Stuart Beck, Stuart Blower, Stuart Forbes, Studio di Ingegneria Massimo Majowiecki, Su Rogers, Sue McMillan, Sue Ogle, Sung Woo Choi, Supertech Consultants International, Susan Blyth, Susan Rice, Susan Smallcombe, Susana Blanes, Susana de la Rosa, Susana Ribes Garcia, Susana Vega, Susanna Clapham, Susi Platt, Susie Blyth, Swantje Kühn, Swinerton, Sylvia Doria, Syska & Hennessy, Sze-King Kan,T Lawson, Tadashi Arai, Taisuke Yamamoto, Taka Tezuka, Takako Shimada, Takasago Thermal Engineering, Takenaka Corporation, Takero Shimazaki, Tamdown, Tamiko Onozawa, Tanner & Wicks, Tanya Samarasingha, Tarmac Cubitts, Taylor Wimpey, Taylor Woodrow Construction, Taywood Engineering, Team Macarie, Tècnics G3, Terri Blada, Tessa Derry, Tetra Design Services, TG3, The Brown Companies, The Callison Partnership, The Davidson Arts Partnership, The Design Solution, The Seaman Group, The Sinnett Partnership, The SWA Group, Theatre Developments, Thomas Oberhofer, Thomas P. Cox Architects, Thomas Theodosiou, Thomas Weber, Thorne Wheatley Associates, Tia Chim, Tibor Bertok, Tim Boyd, Tim Colquhoun, Tim Inskip, Tim Mason, Tim Oakshott, Tim O'Sullivan, Timothy Carson, Tina Manis, Tina Wilson, Tishman Construction, Tishman Speyer Properties, Tito Canella, Tobi Frenzen, Toby Jeavons, Toda Corporation, Tokyo Tatemono, TOLK Services, Tom Alexander, Tom Holberton, Tom Lacey, Tom Nugent, Tom Teatum, Tomás Llamas, Tony Dugdale, Tony Hutt, Torsten Burkhardt, Tosan Popo, Toscano Clements Taylor, Toshiba Elevator & Building Systems Corp., Townsend Landscape Architects, TP Associates, TPS, TPS Schal, Tracy Meller, Travers Morgan, Treadwell & Rollo, Triinu Tubli, Troika Project Management, Turner & Townsend, Ullrich Adami, Ulrike Seifritz, Umezawa Design Office, Umezawa Structural Engineers, URS Corporation, Ute Werner, Van Deusen & Associates, Vanina Mannu, VDA Group, Valentina Vescovi, Veena Parmar, Verónica van Kesteren , Veronika Gliwa, Veronique Letellier, Vicki MacGregor, Vicky Smith, Victor Garcia , Victoria Cambridge, Vidal Fernandez Diez, Vidal y Asociados arquitectos , Vin Goodwin, Violette de la Salle, Virgin Mega Store, Viridain Energy & Environmental, Vivien Morrison, VJ Associates, VJ Mendoza, VK Engineering, VK Studio, Waagner Biro, Walter Zbinden, Warrington Fire Research, Waterman BuildingServices, Waterman Environmental, Waterman Gore, Waterman Partnership, Wates Limited, Watsons Steel, Webb and Tapley, Weidlinger Assocites, Weiske & Partner, Wembley International, Wendy Cheeseman, Wendy Judd, Werner Lang, West 8, Westbury Steel, Wheeler Group Consultancy, Whitby Bird, Whitelaw Turkington, Wietske Meijor, Wiles Mensch, Will Clayton, Will Pryce, Will Thorne, Will Wimshurst, William Carmen, William Firebrace, William Logan, Wirtz International, Wolff Olins, Wolfgang Wagener, Wood Newton, Woods Hardwick, Woolf Construction, WR Davidge & Partners, WSP Cantor Seinuk, WSP Group, WSP Kenchington Ford, WT Partnership, Yamaha Music Foundation, Yamashita Sekkei, Yann Briand, Yann Salmon, Yashar Architects, Yasmin Al-Ani Spence, Yasu Yada, Yasuko Kobayashi, Yolles Partnership, Yoon Choi, Yoshi Uchiyama, Yoshiharu Katoh, Yoshiki Shinohara, Yoshimori Watanabe, Young-In Oh, Yr Gudmundsdottir, YRM Engineers, Yu Shing Sai, Yui Tezuka, Yuji Iwahashi, Yuli Toh.

CREDITS

The publishers would like to thank

Editorial Contributions Renzo Piano, Sir Nicholas Serota and Deyan Sudjic **Design** Al Rodger and David Tanguy **Design Consultant** Ab Rogers **Graphic Consultant** Asuka Kawabata **Project Management** Vicki Macgregor **Editorial Co-ordination** Paul Stelmaszczyk **Directors at Rogers Stirk Harbour + Partners** Richard Rogers, Graham Stirk, Ivan Harbour, Andrew Morris, Mike Davies, Lennart Grut, Richard Paul, Mark Darbon, Amarjit Kalsi and Ian Birtles **All Architects, Modelmakers and Support Staff** – past and present – who have been or are currently associated with Rogers Stirk Harbour + Partners **And All Sponsors** of the exhibition, 'Richard Rogers + Architects: From the House to the City.'

Picture credits

Introduction (p.8): 1 © Fototeca Ltd., photo: Katsuhisa Kida; 2 © Dan Stevens; **Exposed** (pp.13 – 17): Stills from 'Exposed' film: © Rogers Stirk Harbour + Partners, film direction: Marina Willer & Seonaid Mackay, production: Beatrice Vears; **Early Works** (pp.22 – 27): Stills from 'Early Works' film: © Rogers Stirk Harbour + Partners, film direction and production: hijack; **Rogers' House** (pp. 28 – 33): 1 © Rogers Stirk Harbour + Partners; 2 – 5 © Arcaid, photo: Richard Einzig; 6 © Rogers Stirk Harbour + Partners, photo: Richard Rogers; 7 © Arcaid, photo: Richard Einzig; 8 – 12 © Richard Powers / Powerhouse sarl; **Zip-Up House** (pp.34 – 35): 1 – 3 © Rogers Stirk Harbour + Partners; 4 – 6 © Rogers Stirk Harbour + Partners, photo: Eamonn O'Mahony; **Pompidou Centre** (pp.40 – 49): 1 © Rogers Stirk Harbour + Partners; 2 © Corbis, photo: Yann-Arthus Bertrand; 3 – 7 © Rogers Stirk Harbour + Partners; 8 – 11 © Centre Pompidou, photo: Bernard Vincent; 12 © Rogers Stirk Harbour + Partners, photo: John Short; 13 © Arcaid, photo: Richard Einzig; 14 © Paul Wakefield; 15 © Rogers Stirk Harbour + Partners, photo: John Short; **National Gallery Extension** (pp.50 – 53): 1 – 6 © Rogers Stirk Harbour + Partners; **Tokyo International Forum** (pp.54 – 55): 1 – 2 © Rogers Stirk Harbour + Partners, photo: Eamonn O'Mahony; 3 – 4 © Rogers Stirk Harbour + Partners; **South Bank Centre** (pp.56 – 59): 1 – 2 © Rogers Stirk Harbour + Partners; 3 – 4 © Rogers Stirk Harbour + Partners, photo: Hayes Davidson; **Rome Congress Centre** (pp.60 – 61): 1 © Rogers Stirk Harbour + Partners; 2 – 3 © Rogers Stirk Harbour + Partners, photo: Eamonn O'Mahony; **Maggie's London** (pp.62 – 67): 1 – 2 © Arcaid, photo: Richard Bryant; 3 © Rogers Stirk Harbour + Partners; 4 – 7 © Arcaid, photo: Richard Bryant; **Lloyd's of London** (pp.72 – 81): 1 – 4 © Rogers Stirk Harbour + Partners; 5 – 6 © Arcaid, photo: Richard Bryant; 7 RIBA / John Donat; 8 Unknown; 9 – 11 © Rogers Stirk Harbour + Partners, photo: Stephen Le Roith; 12 – 13 © Arcaid, photo: Richard Bryant; 14 © Janet Gill Photography, photo: Janet Gill (courtesy of Alan Trott); 15 © Morley von Sternberg; 16 © Arcaid, photo: Richard Bryant; **Kabuki-Cho** (pp.82 – 85): 1 © Rogers Stirk Harbour + Partners; 2 – 5 © Fototeca Ltd., photo: Katsuhisa Kida; 6 © Rogers Stirk Harbour + Partners, photo: Masaaki Seyiya; 7 © Fototeca Ltd., photo: Katsuhisa Kida; **Tomigaya Exhibition Building** (pp.86 – 87): 1 – 3 © Rogers Stirk Harbour + Partners; **INMOS Microprocessor Factory** (pp.92 – 95): 1 – 3 © Rogers Stirk Harbour + Partners; 4 – 7 © Ken Kirkwood; **Michael Elias House** (pp.96 – 97): 1 – 3 © Rogers Stirk Harbour + Partners; 4 – 5 © Rogers Stirk Harbour + Partners, photo: Eamonn O'Mahony; **Designer Retail Outlet Centre** (pp.98 – 99): 1 © Grant Smith; 2 © Countrywide Photographic, photo: Martin Apps; 3 © Rogers Stirk Harbour + Partners; 4 – 6 © Grant Smith; **Millennium Dome** (pp.102 – 109): 1 © Rogers Stirk Harbour + Partners; 2 © Grant Smith; 3 Unknown; 4 Rogers Stirk Harbour + Partners, photo: Alison Samson; 5 © Grant Smith; 6 © Rogers Stirk Harbour + Partners; 7 © Rogers Stirk Harbour + Partners; 8 © Grant Smith; **ARAM Module** (pp.114 – 117): 1 – 4 © Rogers Stirk Harbour + Partners; **Inland Revenue Headquarters** (pp.118 – 119): 1 © Rogers Stirk Harbour + Partners, photo: Eamonn O'Mahony; 2 – 3 © Rogers Stirk Harbour + Partners; **Turbine Tower** (pp.120 – 121): 1 – 3 © Rogers Stirk Harbour + Partners; **Bordeaux Law Courts** (pp.122 – 129): 1 Rogers Stirk Harbour + Partners – archival photo; 2 Rogers Stirk Harbour + Partners – archival photo; 3 – 6 © Rogers Stirk Harbour + Partners; 7 – 10 © Fototeca Ltd., photo: Katsuhisa Kida; 11 © Christian Richters; 12 © Rogers Stirk Harbour + Partners; 13 © Christian Richters; **National Assembly for Wales** (pp.136 – 141): 1 © Fototeca Ltd., photo: Katsuhisa Kida; 2 – 4 © Rogers Stirk Harbour + Partners; 5 – 6 © Fototeca Ltd., photo: Katsuhisa Kida; 7 © Rogers Stirk Harbour + Partners; **Antwerp Law Courts** (pp.142 – 145): 1 – 2 © Rogers Stirk Harbour + Partners; 3 – 4 © Fototeca Ltd., photo: Katsuhisa Kida; 5 © Grant Smith; 6 © Fototeca Ltd., photo: Katsuhisa Kida; **Mossbourne Community Academy** (pp.146 – 149): 1 © Arcaid, photo: David Churchill; 2 – 3 © Rogers Stirk Harbour + Partners; 4 – 6 © Arcaid, photo: David Churchill; **Channel 4 Television Headquarters** (pp.154 – 159): 1 – 5 © Arcaid, photo: Richard Bryant; 6 © Rogers Stirk Harbour + Partners; 7 © Arcaid, photo: Richard Bryant; **88 Wood Street** (pp.160 – 167): 1 © Rogers Stirk Harbour + Partners; 2 © Sector Light; 3 – 4 © Rogers Stirk Harbour + Partners; 5 © Rogers Stirk Harbour + Partners, photo: Eamonn O'Mahony; 6 – 8 © Fototeca Ltd., photo: Katsuhisa Kida; 9 © Rogers Stirk Harbour + Partners; 10 © Fototeca Ltd., photo: Katsuhisa Kida; 11 © Sector Light; **Lloyd's Register of Shipping** (pp.168 – 173): 1 – 2 © Rogers Stirk Harbour + Partners; 3 © Fototeca Ltd., photo: Katsuhisa Kida; 4 © Grant Smith; 5 © Rogers Stirk Harbour + Partners; 6 © Grant Smith; 7 – 9 © Fototeca Ltd., photo: Katsuhisa Kida; **Terminal 5, Heathrow Airport** (pp.178 – 185): 1 © Rogers Stirk Harbour + Partners; 2 © Fototeca Ltd., photo: Katsuhisa Kida; 3 © Arcaid, photo: Morley von Sternberg; 4 – 6 © Rogers Stirk Harbour + Partners; 7 – 8 © Arcaid, photo: Morley von Sternberg; 9 – 11 © Fototeca Ltd., photo: Katsuhisa Kida; 12 © Rogers Stirk Harbour + Partners, photo: John Short; **Industrialised Housing System** (pp.186 – 189): 1 © Rogers Stirk Harbour + Partners; 2 © Rogers Stirk Harbour + Partners, photo: Eamonn O'Mahony; 3 – 7 © Rogers Stirk Harbour + Partners; **Terminal 4, Barajas Airport** (pp.190 – 199): 1 © Rogers Stirk Harbour + Partners; 2 © Amparo Garrido; 3 © Rogers Stirk Harbour + Partners, photo: MAC Fotografica; 4 © Amparo Garrido; 5 © Arcaid, photo: Richard Bryant; 6 © Rogers Stirk Harbour + Partners, photo: Simon Smithson; 7 © Fototeca Ltd., photo: Katsuhisa Kida; 8 – 10 © Rogers Stirk Harbour + Partners; 11 © Fototeca Ltd., photo: Katsuhisa Kida; 12 © Arcaid, photo: Richard Bryant; 13 © Duccio Malagamba; 14 © Amparo Garrido; **Bodegas Protos** (pp.200 – 205): 1 © VIEW Pictures Limited, photo: Paul Raftery; 2 © Rogers Stirk Harbour + Partners; 3 © Rainer Schlautmann; 4 © Rogers Stirk Harbour + Partners; 5 © Rogers Stirk Harbour + Partners; 6 – 8 © VIEW Pictures Limited, photo: Paul Raftery; 9 – 10 © Fototeca Ltd., photo: Katsuhisa Kida; **Coin Street** (pp.210 – 213): 1 – 7. © Rogers Stirk Harbour + Partners; **London as it could be** (pp.214 – 219): 1 – 10 © Rogers Stirk Harbour + Partners; **Shanghai Pudong Masterplan** (pp.220 – 225): 1 – 7 © Rogers Stirk Harbour + Partners; **The Leadenhall Building** (pp.232 – 233): 1 © Rogers Stirk Harbour + Partners; 2 © Cityscape; **Canary Wharf** (pp.234 – 235): 1 – 3 © Rogers Stirk Harbour + Partners; R9 Station (pp.236 – 237): 1 – 2 © Rogers Stirk Harbour + Partners; 3 – 4 © Fototeca Ltd., photo: Katsuhisa Kida; **One Hyde Park** (pp.238 – 239): 1 – 2 © Hayes Davidson (John MacLean); **Ching Fu Group Headquarters** (pp.240 – 241): 1 © Fototeca Ltd., photo: Katsuhisa Kida, 2 – 3 © Rogers Stirk Harbour + Partners; **Metropolitana Linea 1 – Santa Maria del Pianto** (p.242): 1 – 2 © Rogers Stirk Harbour + Partners; **Parc1** (p.243): 1 – 2 © Rogers Stirk Harbour + Partners; **Barangaroo** (pp.244 – 245): 1 – 2 © Rogers Stirk Harbour + Partners; **Design for Manufacture Housing** (pp.246 – 251): 1 – 2 © Rogers Stirk Harbour + Partners, 3 © Fototeca Ltd., photo: Katsuhisa Kida, 4 © Rogers Stirk Harbour + Partners, 5 – 7 © Fototeca Ltd., photo: Katsuhisa Kida; **NEO Bankside** (pp.252 – 253): 1 – 2 © Rogers Stirk Harbour + Partners; **World Conservation and Exhibitions Centre, British Museum** (pp.254 – 255): 1 © Hayes Davidson, 2 – 3 © Rogers Stirk Harbour + Partners; **Grand Paris** (pp.256 – 257): 1 – 3 © Rogers Stirk Harbour + Partners; **Da-An Park** (p.258): 1 © Rogers Stirk Harbour + Partners; **Grand Hotel** (p.259): 1 – 2 © Rogers Stirk Harbour + Partners; **Tadawul – Saudi Stock Exchange** (pp.260 – 261): 1 © Hayes Davidson; 2 © Rogers Stirk Harbour + Partners; **GyeongGi Do Provincial Government Offices** (pp.262 – 263): 1 – 4 © Rogers Stirk Harbour + Partners; **Inside Out** (pp. 264 – 271): Stills from 'Inside Out' film: direction: Marina Willer, production: Beatrice Vears, photography: Jonathan Clabburn & Melissa Duarte.

Gatefold Section (pp.130 – 135): **Science campus project**; © Rogers Stirk Harbour + Partners; **Pill Creek**: © Arcaid; **Creek Vean**: © Arcaid; **Reliance Controls**: © Foster + Partners; **Rogers' House**: © Arcaid, photo: Richard Bryant; **Zip-Up House**: © Rogers Stirk Harbour + Partners; **ARAM**: © Rogers Stirk Harbour + Partners; **Pompidou Centre**: © Corbis, photo: Yann-Arthus Bertrand; **B&B Italia Offices**: © Domus, photo: Giorgio Casali; **UOP Factory**: © Richard Einzig; **Lloyd's of London**: © Arcaid, photo: Richard Bryant; **Fleetguard Factory**: © Ken Kirkwood; **Coin Street**: © Rogers Stirk Harbour + Partners; **National Gallery Extension**: © Rogers Stirk Harbour + Partners; **PA Technology**: © Ken Kirkwood; **PA Technology**: © Ken Kirkwood; **London As It Could Be**: © Rogers Stirk Harbour + Partners; **Kabuki-Cho**: © Fototeca Ltd., photo: Katsuhisa Kida; **European Court of Human Rights**: © Fototeca Ltd., photo: Katsuhisa Kida, **Terminal 5, Heathrow Airport**: © Morley von Sternberg, **Toyko International Forum**: © Rogers Stirk Harbour + Partners; **Tomigaya Exhibition Building**: © Rogers Stirk Harbour + Partners; **Channel 4 Television Headquarters**: © Arcaid, photo: Richard Bryant; **Michael Elias House**: © Rogers Stirk Harbour + Partners; **Industrial Housing System**: © Eamonn O'Mahony; **Inland Revenue Headquarters**: © Rogers Stirk Harbour + Partners, photo: Eamonn O'Mahony; **Turbine Tower**: © Rogers Stirk Harbour + Partners; **Shanghai Pudong Masterplan**: © Rogers Stirk Harbour + Partners; **Bordeaux Law Courts**: © Christian Richterss; **South Bank Centre**: © Hayes Davidson; **88 Wood Street**: Sector Light; **Lloyd's Register of Shipping**: © Fototeca Ltd., photo: Katsuhisa Kida; **Minami Yamashiro Elementary School**: © Fototeca Ltd., photo: Katsuhisa Kida; **Paddington Basin Grand Union**: © Eamonn O'Mahony; **Las Arenas**: © Rogers Stirk Harbour + Partners; **Canary Wharf**: © Rogers Stirk Harbour + Partners; **Torre Espacio**: © Rogers Stirk Harbour + Partners; **Maggie's London**: © Morley von Sternberg; **Sabadell Congress and Cultural Centre**: © Rogers Stirk Harbour + Partners; **Barcelona and L'Hospitalet Law Courts**: © Rogers Stirk Harbour + Partners; **Mossbourne Community Academy**: © Arcaid, photo: David Churchill; **Parc1**: © Rogers Stirk Harbour + Partners; **Silvercup West Studios**: © Rogers Stirk Harbour + Partners; **The Leadenhall Building**: © Cityscape; **R9 Station**: © Rogers Stirk Harbour + Partners; **Bodegas Protos**: © VIEW Pictures Limited, photo: Paul Raftery; **One Hyde Park**: © Hayes Davidson; **Ching Fu Headquarters**: © Fototeca Ltd., photo: Katsuhisa Kida; **Barangaroo**: © Rogers Stirk Harbour + Partners; **Design for Manufacture Housing**: © Fototeca Ltd., photo: Katsuhisa Kida; **Palmas Altas Centre for Technology**: © Mark Bentley; **Metropolitiana Linea 1 – Santa Maria**: © Rogers Stirk Harbour + Partners; **World Conservation and Exhibition Centre, British Museum**: © Rogers Stirk Harbour + Partners, **P7, Campus de la Justicia de Madrid**: © Rogers Stirk Harbour + Partners; **Grand Paris**: © Rogers Stirk Harbour + Partners; **NEO Bankside**: © Rogers Stirk Harbour + Partners; **Centro Internacional**: © 7T, photo: Chris Curtis; **Da-An Park**: © Rogers Stirk Harbour + Partners; **Far Glory**: © Rogers Stirk Harbour + Partners; **Tadawul – Saudi Stock Exchange**: © Rogers Stirk Harbour + Partners; **GyeongGi Do Provincial Government Offices**: © Rogers Stirk Harbour + Partners; **Grand Hotel**: © Rogers Stirk Harbour + Partners. All portrait photographs used in gatefold section: © Rogers Stirk Harbour + Partners (except image of John Young, Richard Rogers, Mike Davies etc: © Patrick Shanahan / The Telegraph).

Note: The Publishers would like to personally thank all the photographers who have kindly allowed their work to be reproduced in this publication. We have endeavoured to respect the rights of third parties and if any rights have been overlooked in individual cases, the mistake will be correspondingly amended where possible.